WICCA BOOK OF SPELLS

THE ULTIMATE BOOK OF SHADOWS FOR THE SOLITARY PRACTITIONER. A GUIDE FOR BEGINNER WICCANS, WITCHES, PAGANS AND PRACTITIONERS OF MAGIC.

ATHENA CROWLEY

Table of contents

Introduction

As children we are often told fairy tales and tales of magic, these stories stick with us throughout our lives. Yet have you ever caught yourself wondering about the magic that may exist around you? What form this could take, how does the wind blow through the trees? What makes the sunshine, the moon glow and allows for that magic connection we feel inside when we see someone we love? These questions are often the initial questions of those whom discover Wicca or develop an interest in the craft.

Wicca, also lovingly called "the Old Religion" by many adepts, is a collection of beliefs from ancient pagan cultures, folklore, native traditions combined with elements of modern-day science, health and psychic wisdom. Often only referred to as witchcraft or *the craft*. According to several American and British surveys, the Wiccan way is the fastest growing religious belief in the world. Heralding from a wealth of various belief systems and traditions ultimately encouraging its practitioners to find their own unique expression and, most importantly, harmonious connection within life. For unlike the tales of witches we may hear as children or know stories of from the middle ages, a Wiccan practitioner is someone whom has dedicated their life to exploring the divine reality of the natural universe through opening one's self fully to truth and unconditional love. Through the understanding that their own inner wisdom and connection to nature or ability to listening to the cosmos a witch is one who, by tradition, looks to use the ways of magic to bring love and truth into all walks of life, never to harm another. We are even shown this oath of truth and love within the Wiccan Rede, a sacred Wiccan text with the following vow:

> Bide the Wiccan Law, ye must.
> In perfect love and perfect trust
> Eight words the Wiccan Rede fulfill:
> An ye none harm, do as ye will.

So, as we embark on this exploration into the realms of Wicca and its way of being, we will explore the connections to nature this tradition calls upon, we will need to understand the truths around magic, folklore and even the routes of this ancient tradition. From here you will begin to see for yourself how this century old religion has already become one of the fastest growing belief systems in the world and even learn the tools to embark on this journey of magic for yourself.

Wicca first came into the public eye in the early 19th Century. Whilst its true origins are still debated, even within modern Wiccan covens themselves. Gerald Gardner, also referred to as Scire, is known as the father of Wicca. Yet, according to Gardner he was but a man who brought this ancient wisdom out of the shadows and into the public eye to repave the way for what he always referred as the ways of Old, or the Craft, even today adepts still use these names. This wisdom has been passed down for millennia through a hidden lineage of witchcraft. For the word Wicca, itself comes from the Anglo-Saxon word for 'wise one.' Gardner himself also pulls teachings, wisdom and methods of life from native cultures, ancient traditions and even the elusive New Forest coven that he was initiated into in 1939. Whilst many have tried no one has found concrete evidence of Scire's New Forest coven, as they were a secret Rosicrucian Order. However, whether Wicca was the birth of Gardner's own path or in fact a lineage passed down through the shadows, this does not stop many followers from practicing the forms of magic in daily life. In fact, this mysterious origin even works holds alluring value to some of its members.

This debate of its origins Wicca over the past century has seen many changes and evolutions with smaller covens being formed that have their own beliefs as to the origins. Yet there are some foundational beliefs that can be found throughout, of truth and love. Gardner originally began the Bricket Wood Coven, upon leaving the New Forest Coven, in hopes to bring the Wiccan way to the public eye. Yet of course he was not alone in bringing this way of being into the public eye. Along with the aid of witches such as Doreen Valiente, who served as Gardner's high priestess, together the two wrote the Gardnerian Book of Shadows.

This book of shadows was heavily influenced by Scire's own experiences, influences and insights and paved the way to be the foundation of many modern-day Book of Shadows. Originally Gardner had written this book himself and sought Valiente's assistance to refine the book and help to spread its teachings. The book itself called upon occultist teachings from the later 19th Century as well as many teachings and knowledge of the 13th Century (which these original 13th Century teachings called upon even more ancient knowledge again). One such presence that could be found in this Book of Shadows was the wisdom and practices of Aleister Crowley, an early 20th Century British Occultist. Yet Doreen felt the teachings of Aleister Crowley were to heavily associate with black magic, or magick as Crowley often spelled it, for many people and began to remove most of Crowley's influence from the Gardner Book of Shadows. Over time disputes such as this would eventually lead the two to go their separate ways. With Doreen going onto start her own coven as would several other members of the Bricket Wood coven. Yet each Wiccan would ultimately take with them some of the elements from Gardner's coven, filtering it down through the traditions that have led to our current understanding of Wicca.

Throughout the following decades Wicca would spread not only through the UK but eventually reach the shores of America and Australia also. This was due to the dedicated practice, involvement and influence of 20th Century occultists such as Robert Cochrane and Raymond Buckland, not to mention Scire's original coven members and colleagues Lois Bourne and Patricia Crowther. As some of the pioneers for the craft each having their own strong influence on the path and forming their own covens for the Wiccan way to truly expand throughout all corners of the globe over the last 90 years. We begin to see a spiritual lineage shrouded by mystery, wisdom and magic that one could truly never wish to put into words.

Infamously known within the Wiccan world, yet still playing such a large role is Robert Cochrane. It was Cochrane who started many covens, that continued to disband and have falling out for various reasons. Yet his dedication and devotion to the craft led him to continuously form covens and bring Wiccans together. Claiming that his family had been witches and practitioners of the craft since the 17th Century. We see through Cochranes story and path the strong association of family lineage that many Wiccans connect with even today. With the claim that his Aunty guided him through the craft, and his father was a secret practitioner who had learn from his grandfather before him, Cochrane also introduced many new concepts to the growing Wiccan tradition. Including worship to Hekate, or the Horned God and referring to Gardner's Goddess as the "White Goddess" we still see strong evidence of Cochranes influence within the craft.

It was even within Cochranes second coven, the Clan of Tubal Cain, that Doreen Valiente would seek refuge for some time after abandoning Gardner's coven. For Robert was known as one of Gardner's many rivals in the craft, yet often thought of as the most influential of them all. Through this period Cochrane was known to mock many of the Gardnerian practices and traditions whilst heralding in his own traditions. Including the addition of his five main ritual tools, that varied from already known traditions, such as the ritual knife, a staff referred to as a *stang,* a cup or chalice, a stone (to sharpen ones ritual knife), and a ritual cord that must be worn by coven members. Yet this newfound friendship between Valiente and Cochrane would also be short lived but would leave Valiente to write about her experiences with Robert Cochrane in years to come.

Cochrane was also known to the first coven to drop the Book of Shadows in favor for working from merely knowledge that he called "a more traditional way of doing things." These alternative methods did initially draw in many new members and initiates onto the Wiccan path, yet each in time would come to go their own way after various falling outs or grievances with Cochranes outward opinions and often proved false claims that formed his craft.

With all this in mind however following his death, which was self-induced, many of Cochranes traditions and ways were adopted by Wiccans in the decades to follow and even form much of the diversity we experience in modern Wicca as it is today. Through his own demise witches and practitioners that he had initiated into the craft would go on to write their own books, such as Evan John Jones, which would revitalize his alternative view of the craft. For whilst Robert Cochrane did not publish any completed books of his own throughout his life, several were written from his notes, students and collected writings after his death. This in turn would ultimately earn him the title, according to many, as the *"Father of Traditional Witchcraft."*

As for Doreen Valiente, we can begin to see how her path continues to wind through various stages of the newly developing Wiccan way. Through her various experiences with both Gardner and Cochrane, Valiente would go on to write 9 books herself about that would truly open the Wiccan realms to the public eye. Some of these titles included the likes of *Where Witchcraft Lives, Natural Magic, The Rebirth of the Witchcraft and Witchcraft Tomorrow.* With this passion and dedication to the craft it is no wonder that many people honor Valiente as one of the most influential people in the development of Witchcraft as we know it today.

With her background as starting ceremonial magic and occult practices as a teenager, it did not take long for Doreen to dive into the emerging realms of Wiccan and play this pivotal role. Aside from joining Gardner's first coven, and Cochranes second, Doreen also started her own coven for a short period in between these two covens, that still adopted many of Gardner' s Bricket Coven traditions, just without Wiccan laws, that she believed were of Scire's own creation. Yet even after disbanding and starting her own coven separate of Gardner, it was her loyalty to him that also would lead her to leave Cochrane in the future.

Many people spoke highly of the charm that Doreen Valiente had as she moved throughout the developing Wiccan world. One can still find praise for Valiente within the modern Wiccan world, as her works are still believed to be some of the most authentic and knowledgeable material of the craft. Even Gardner himself known to say he would have never been anywhere near as successful at promoting Wicca if it were not for Valiente's help and dedication. Loved and still honored by many, much to her distaste, Valiente is known as the "Mother of Wicca" or "Mother of Modern Witchcraft."

Of course, these are but merely examples of the colorful foundation of Wicca and the way in which it began to emerge from the shadows. One could easily continue to dive into this history and follow the thousands of covens that would eventually come to be what we refer to as Wicca today. Yet regardless of which view one takes, or how one comes on to the path the understanding and respect for "Old ways," how old they truly are is the disputed factor, is universal through all traditions. With each path finding their own story to justify the means, we still find many similarities in the spells and magic that unfolds in the craft. Hence the purpose of the pages to come, with the vision to honor any tradition you may follow, herald from or have the passion to discover the spells and knowledge held within are for the benefit of all witches and Wiccans alike. With the vision that we may keep the old way alive and still deeper our connection in truth and love as was the vision of the founding pioneers before us, that each dedicated their lives to share their truth as was seen through their light. As you continue through this book this is what I wish to pass onto you, may you hold an open mind, an open heart and may you open the magic within to find your own truth. Keep what resonates for you and for your own path on the way to truth, leave behind that which is meant for another and adapt that which you can to perfect and transform this into wisdom to share with any being that may cross you own path. In this way we can each grow in truth, love and unity as we cultivate knowledge and magic, to truly embody the fullest meaning of becoming *a wise one or Wicca.*

Chapter 1: The types of Wiccan Magic

As a witch or practitioner of the Wiccan way it is important to know your craft. For as we are beginning to explore the Wiccan way is a broad and open expression of connecting with the true nature of life. Through forming a relationship with the elements, nature and the cosmos both on a microcosmic and macrocosmic scale. Often aligning through magic rituals, ceremonies and magic spells a Wiccan can connect to this truth. Yet when we first step onto the path we are faced with questions like; what exactly is magic? How do we practice or use magic? Is there only one form or type of magic? These are often the first questions for an initiate on the path, and the honest answer is there is not one simple answer. On the contrary, we find a large world waiting to be discovered. For as we have begun to see the Wiccan way is combinations of many pagan traditions, ancient wisdom, various cultural knowledge and even religious or scientific philosophy all pulled together. This is where the realms of magic can become an exciting and magical exploration in of itself, before we even begin to harness the magic of life.

So, as we dive into exploring the various forms of magic and their use, let us simply set a foundation. Within all types of magic there are two common components; for magic is the artform of channeling the universal energy around you and within you to shape and manifest your intention into reality. In more mystical words, magic is the word of making dreams come true. This leaves our two main components of a strong intent and a way to amplify this intent. From here the main difference in types of magic is the element we connect with to amplify this intent or the method behind our manifestation. Now as we explore the various types of magic, understand that there is no set right or wrong forms, nor do you need even only practice one form yet you can also combine many types of magic because this is your path and your intent that is the other key ingredient to our the craft. Some witch's do have their favorite type of spellcasting, whilst others dabble in multiple practice, experiment for yourself and watch the magic unfold.

High Magic & Ceremonial Magic

Ceremonial Magic or *High Magic* are the most common names for this form of the craft. This tradition is highly connected to the Ways of Old, using many elaborate, intricate or formal rituals, symbols, rules or tools to cast spells. Many witch's regard this as the most 'Occult' practice of magic. The purposes of this form of magic are often aimed at spiritual growth and connection to the higher realms, so we find much of this ceremonial magic is based on the Kabballah and alchemical practices.

As many forms of high magic are based around philosophical or esoteric practices, it is common that this form of magic lies within orders that call for initiation; such as freemasonry, Hermetic Studies, Templars, Society of Light or Golden Dawn to name a few. This form of magic can be a powerful and potent tool for the initiate that is wishing to deepen their connections with otherworldly entities or spiritual realms. Just be aware that this is a very precise form and it is best to seek initiation into the Craft to really tap into the powers of old.

Low Magic & Earth Magic

Whilst called Earth Magic or Low Magic, this is no less powerful than High Magic and can still be about spiritual growth yet is named thus as it is generally more mundane and magic relating to every-day life. This form of magic is often known as a more instinctual form of magic. Low magic gives more room for creativity than the strict rules of High magic and can be performed with and without rituals. Sometimes referred to throughout Wicca as *Folk Magic,* so named as it is the magic of common folk, was often passed down through family tradition and folklore. With uses of this craft often based around simple charms and basic ritual beliefs that may have a very practical grounded essence. One may call upon this form of magic for the survival of family, friends or even self-preservation. Within Folklore this is the form of magic that was said to secure a good harvest, a partner or child and protect from misfortune and sickness or death. Thus, despite the name of low magic, this is a more common form with the Wiccan traditions than that of high magic. For example, one may draw a hex sign on the entrance to their home to ward off evil spirits, create a circle of lavender around the bed for a positive and peaceful night sleep, or even mutter a chant of healing over a cut or burn. This is very subtle yet powerful form of grounded magic giving room for spontaneity in the craft.

Natural Magic & Elemental Magic

Possibly the most common form of magic heralding from the Druids, Shamans, Medicine Women, Healers and the Ways of Old. *Natural Magic* or *Elemental Magic* gains its name from being a form of witchcraft that deals with any magic that calls upon the natural elements in spells, or even the working with magical tools and symbols that represent the sacred elements. This can often be categorized with forms of Folk Magic or Low Magic, as it can be practiced anytime, anywhere without the need for intensive preparation. This magic is very intuitively based, and some traditions even say you need not cast a circle for these workings!

Wicca calls upon this form of natural magic for a large array of spellcraft and ceremonies. One may connect with this way of magic through crystals, nature, the weather and seasons or using tools like candle magic, herbals magic, rune magic, moon and planetary magic. This is a common component of kitchen magic, as we are connecting with the elements through our food. Even musical and color magic fall under the umbrella of Natural magic. This is what allows it to be the most common form. Hence, also making it the perfect type of magic to incorporate into one's own path, either at the beginning stages or even further down the path. Elemental Magic is a way to always take magic with you, as you only need a connection to nature. These of course are a broad outlook on Elemental/ Natural magic and each Wiccan tradition has its own outlook on what would be defined this way, yet this shows the diversity that lay within the Wiccan approach.

Planetary Magic & Moon Magic

Planetary Magic or *Moon Magic* is heavily based upon the age-old tradition and science of Astrology. This craft called upon the knowledge of the Sun, Moon and stars within our Solar system, thus sometimes referred to as lunar and solar magic in various traditions. To connect with this practice of magic one needs to have a strong understanding of not only Astrology but also Astronomy and how these two are related. When we begin to understand this form of magic we begin understanding and connecting to the macrocosm rather than just seeing the microcosm of our existence. Moon Astrology in its most simplistic form is based around the moon phases making this a balance of natural magic and planetary magic, showing us how types of magic are constantly overlapping. However, this form of magic takes a lot of planning and often requires the foresight of the astrological tides to perform rituals, ceremonies and spells at the exact moment to harness the power of the planets with our intent to bring our goal into manifestation. There are many books, and resources relating to this form of magic, that can quickly become a life-long path of understanding to the cosmos for the Moon Witch wishing to connect with the greater cosmic influence on our daily existence. Which with the right understanding and connection one can even call upon this form of magic in divination as a tool for insight and foresight on one's life path, to navigate the path of life.

Chaos Magic

Connected to altered states of consciousness or Gnosis, Chaos Magic, calls upon drawing energy from our psyche to manipulate our spellcraft. This form of magic takes practice and connection to a deep meditative state to be able to understand how to call forth this energy from our psyche to effectively charge our spells with energy. Many cultures have practiced this form of spellcasting throughout the ages by reaching these states of altered consciousness through ritualistic dance, sexual intercourse, physical exertion or transcendental meditation. Yet as it is a drawing this energy from your subconscious or super conscious, as some refer to it, one is essentially drawing this energy from the universe into reality and therefore once you can connect with this space it does not take make planning or preparation for spell casting simple openness. Meaning if we can stay in a state of Gnosis, we can access this magic in any place or time, without the need for circles or ceremonial tools.

Known through many Wiccans traditions sigil crafting is the most common practice of chaos magic. Yet there are no set rules to chaos magic, as it is intuitive based rather than intellectual. So many witches will use techniques such as linking sigils, connecting servitors or cut-up techniques. Whichever way you practice this form of chaos magic it is always advised to proceed slowly and with caution as this is a potentially powerful practice when performed correctly and one can often be surprised by the outcomes of their spell work. So be careful what you wish for!

Summoning Magic

If you wish to have higher beings, spirits or energies bring you intent into reality you first need to cultivate a relationship with them, and this comes through the practice of summoning magic. This is the practice of calls upon the energy from entities from other planes of consciousness into our spellcraft. Whether this be The God or Goddess energy, a connection to the Faeries, Spirit animals, Elementals or Ancestors this is a form of devotional magic found in many Wiccan traditions. Hence it is important to first develop a relationship with these entities. Patience in developing this relationship is often the first component of this form of spellcraft. Once we have formed this relationship there are many rituals, ceremonies and spells used to summon an entity into our circle. As we are not always sure which energy or entity we are calling in many Wiccans believe a circle is a must within form of spellcraft, to ensure the purity of the work. Pagans and Wicca tradition have called upon summoning spells since the ways of old as the most powerful way to connect with spirit guides, knowing the right guide will chose you.

Divination Magic

Debated amongst various Wiccan traditions if this is its own form of magic or simply a component of all types of magic. Divination is the art of connecting to the Divine to gain insight into the future or gain clarity on the path that may lie ahead. For it is known that the future is not set in stone, yet many possible paths may lie ahead, this form of magic can allow insight and clarity as to which path may serve the best to achieve our desired intent. Some witches will call upon various forms of spells, rituals or ceremonies to divine the future like connecting with the Tarot, tea leaf readings, reading the I-ching or runes to forms of scrying and connecting with pendulums, others may simply receive visions through dreams or meditation. Divination is an open form of the craft found throughout all traditions of Wicca and many pagan traditions alike. Whether you wish to class this as its own form of magic or simply a component to add into your other magical tradition's divination is a powerful way of understanding and navigating one's spiritual path by connecting to the knowledge of your guides moment to moment.

Sympathetic Magic

Sympathetic Magic is commonly used to 'link' a person and object together, so that in time what is to happen to the object will also affect the person. This is often associated with the practice of Hoodoo magic or the concept of Voodoo dolls, which many people know through folklore and myths. This form of magic can be performed with either a poppet or doll yet is also an object that represents the person will suffice for this craft. Whilst this form of magic has been given a reputation with black magic or hexing spells, in reality this is a form of magic to help achieve goals in healing, cultivating love or even spells of prosperity. The Wiccan tradition has passed these secrets down for the last century, keeping most secrets to the art within familiar linages, to keep the intent pure and truthful.

Talismanic Magic

Working with amulets, talismans or other objects that may be charmed this is a form of magic that either draws or repels specific energies to the wearer of said enchanted tool. One may enchant these objects with various intent such as protection, love, abundance or warding off evil and spells of protection. It is always best to choose the object, or amulet that is most conducive to the intent you wish to cultivate, for example, a rose quartz may be used to draw upon love or a sprig of rosemary, or heart necklace may also be used. Whilst, a pouch of basil or vile of patchouli oil as a necklace may be used to call upon abundance. These talisman's can also be man-made objects or objects found within nature. Once infused with the intent and thus enchanted, a talisman would then be carried or worn to activate its magical properties.

These are just some forms of magic that are common within Wiccan traditions. As a witch continues to explore these realms of magic one will surely stumble across many other paths, traditions and forms of the craft that have served the Wiccan way throughout time. One may wish to harness only one type of magic, or more commonly call upon multiple facets of magic to step into the full potential of spellcraft. Take your time to explore and practice with each form of magic, notice what resonates with you and in no time, you will begin to see your connection with the magical realm begin to flourish. You may find that you cultivate a practice with ceremonial magic in a daily prayer or call upon planetary magic at various moon phases in Esbat ceremonies or even connect with folk magic in your home life. Keep your interpretation of magical expression open and allow it to become your unique craft not being limited or contained to one form of witchcraft yet allowing yourself to *be wild and free*.

Chapter 2: Wiccan Tools & Uses

As we begin to grasp the various types of magic, we soon begin to find common tools used throughout the craft. Before we continue our journey into casting the spells themselves let us acknowledge some of the tools that we may call upon. Each tradition is also known to have various tools that they call upon or call by different names so we can not cover all below, whilst some traditions even will have no tools at all. Here are but a handful that we will call upon throughout this book to help start you along the path and to guide you in beginning your own Grimoire.

Athame

Athame is the Wiccan term referring to a ceremonial blade or knife, used within many traditional pagan or Wiccan rituals. Ceremonial blades such as this are often used for spell casting, channeling energy or intent, drawing circles, banishing negativity, amongst a variety of other magical craft. Within Wicca an athame usually, not always, features a black handle and is inscribed with runes, symbols or intention to honor the intent of the individual's practice.

This magical tool is often passed down in the lineage from a relative or adept Wiccan to keep the energy flowing in the tradition. Yet this is not always necessary, when assembling your altar any blade you may have access to can serve as your athame. There is no need to wait for one to be passed down or purchase a new blade. Even a dull old kitchen knife can be cleansed and revitalized into a potent magical tool. For example, if you have a kitchen knife with a wooden handle, you could inscribe it with your own runes onto the handle or embellish the tool with beads or fabric to make it into your unique athame. Within some practices the athame need not only be a knife, but you tool of choice. Meaning even if you are a writer or a painter, perhaps your athame is a ceremonial pen or paintbrush. Whatever tool you choose as your athame, remember this is sacred magical tool and to treat it accordingly to allow for your intent to manifest through this item. Placing it on your altar will also infuse the athame with sacred vibrations.

Besom

The Besom, or broom, is a stereotypical witch's tool throughout the centuries. This is usually a magical tool not for flying away on in the evenings, this myth came from traditional pagan rituals that occur when a newlywed couple is stead-fasting, they would then symbolically fly off on their broom together. Rather a broom or besom is usually a small bundle of twigs tied to a thicker branch that may serve as the brooms handle. Within Wicca and other pagan traditions, brooms are typically used for purifying an area, cleansing rooms, circles, or altars in preparation for rituals and ceremonies. Many Wiccans may have a smaller besom dedicated to cleansing just their altar daily to keep the energies pure and cleansed throughout all periods of the Wheel of Life.

As with all magical tools it is important that this item is sacred and unique to your own practice. Thus, making your own broom can be an excellent introduction into the craft, as well as a good excuse to connect with nature and take a walk through the woods. All one need do is whilst walking in the woods, collect a bundle of small twigs that you feel drawn to, along with one stouter stick that will serve as the handle. Bound the twigs and handle together using twine, thread or another form of natural material is best. There is much folklore around these different materials and their own magical properties, so choose the one that is most in alignment with your own way. Finish with a blessing incantation to set the intent for your besom and add any additional decorations that may personify this tool further for you.

Candles

Candles are often seen on an altar and one of the most commonly used magical tools. Through candle magic one can harness the power of the fire elemental, the element of transformation. Whether this be for specific candle magic, which we will explore shortly, or in offering, used for rituals, ceremonies, invocations, cleansings and many other rites. These powerful tools cast an enchanting dim flickering light that can even be used within times of reflection and rest. Candle magic is one of the simplest practices of spellcasting and doesn't require difficult preparations; a basic example of this is like when you have a birthday and blow out the candle to make a wish, this is a simplistic form of candle magic.

When practicing the craft of candle magic is based on three magical key principals of deciding a goal, visualize the desired result and focus your intent, feeling the vibration of this intent to manifest the result. Essentially one would just increase their intent by using various color candles, shapes or sizes that align with your intent. Some traditions will say the size of the candle does not matter, however as folklore would traditionally say it is bad to burn an old candle for new spells, large and bigger candles can often be counterproductive with the craft as they hold this old energy. This is due to the belief that many Wiccans have that a candle picks up the vibrations of the items in the room around it after it begins to burn. So, it is common within spellcasting that one will use a tea candle or the tine white unscented candles that are about four inches long, as these have the most neutral energy and are perfect for one-time rituals.

Whilst size is a disputed factor in candle magic, color is known to have effect on the intent and potency of the spell. This is often a key component in candle magic, with many rituals or spells calling upon certain colors as part of the practice. Some of the following colors are typically used for the corresponding spells:

- Red- Courage and health, lust and sexual love
- Pink- Sweet love, self-love and friendship
- Orange- Attraction or encouragement
- Gold- Financial gain, solar connections and business ventures
- Green- Wealth, abundance and fertility
- Light Blue- Patience, healing, understanding and well being
- Dark Blue- Vulnerability and depression
- Yellow- Protection or persuasion
- Purple- Power and ambition
- Brown- Earth-related and animal workings
- Black- Banishment/ negativity
- White- Purity, cleansing and truth
- Silver- Reflection, intuition and lunar connections

Again, candle magic is an excellent way to practice spell casting. As you begin to develop these skills you may begin to work with spells that also call upon the combination of candle magic, herbal magic, and invocations all together to enhance the power of these spells.

Incense & Smudging

Throughout Wicca and pagan practices, amidst other cultures and traditions, incense and smudging rituals have been called upon for a variety of magical purposes. Utilizing the fragrant smoke from burning various herbs, incense can also be an enchanting tool to work with. Frequently used by practitioners for cleansing rituals, like cleansing circles or altars, as well as any areas, persons or objects that may hold lingering energy. This can be a powerful tool to invoke during your preparation periods for various ceremonies. Many practitioners also burn incense during rituals or meditation to induce altered states of consciousness to connect with the divine. Whilst we are burning incense or smudging, we are not only creating a nice aroma, that triggers emotional responses and offers a nice mood-setting, we are literally changing the vibration in the atmosphere. We know, as Wiccans, that everything in life has its own vital energy force and vibration. So when you are blending herbs or smudging a space one is combining the vibrational energy of differing magical herbs with the vibration of your intent to effect the vibrations present in the space, thus also impacting not just our material world but also the ethereal worlds around us and within us.

As explored in more depth in my book *Wiccan Herbalism: A Beginners Grimoire* there are many different applications, recipes and rituals for incense and smudging that call upon the powerful magic properties of the herbal kingdom. The exploration of incense can be a lifelong practice from making your own blends of loose-leaf incense, collecting incense sticks or cones, using them to cleanse or cast spells, this is completely up to your own practice, like within all spellcraft a combination can even amplify one's connection to magic. As the symbol of the Air and Fire elementals, some Wiccans class incense and smudging to be a core component to Wiccan tradition, and thus is often used as an adjunct to magic rituals, ceremonies or forms of the craft.

Herbs

Herbs, flowers and plants have always played a strong role within human history and evolution, this role of herbs is also strongly present within the Wiccan traditions. Honored throughout the ages for their various magical healing and protection properties, throughout nearly every culture since the beginning of time, the herbal kingdom has shaped many forms of our modern medicine and is deeply entwined within folklore. Fortunately, many of the secrets behind the vibrational magic of herbs has been passed down throughout the generations and preserved within folklore to still serve us today. Throughout the Wiccan craft we find herbs are a key component to many forms of spell casting, cleansing rituals and merely shaping our reality by their presence alone, according to tradition.

Various Wiccans call upon herbal magic for differing reasons. From simply growing herbs to deepen the connection and honor the cycles of nature, a popular practice of hedge witches, or possibly cooking, brewing and calling upon the culinary magic of herbs, used by kitchen witches, to even the tradition of herbal bundles, jars and pouches for healing, cleansing and protection. The mysteries of the herbal lore have been so infused into our development of spirituality that we often take these powerful tools for granted. Hence, many Wiccan and pagan traditions give offerings to the herbal arts at times of the year through Samhain rituals or Esbat ceremonies. Keeping a selection of herbs, or growing your own witches garden, is recommended in nearly all traditions of Wicca. For these powerful plants may have multiple roles to play in rituals, candle magic, cauldron spells, incense and smudging ceremonies, or even the crafting of their own spell work, as we will see in the coming pages. Even gathering your own herbs from within nature, through practices of wildcrafting, can be a magical way to connect with Gaia, yet do seek the knowledge of an adept forager to be sure you collect the right herbs, as some do come with potent magic that should be explored with caution. Let us have a brief look at some of the common herbs we may cross within the craft:

Chamomile – Used in the craft for healing, sleeping, purification or cleansing rituals. Often used to bring good luck, wealth and good health. Even used to aid in meditation practices.

Lavender—A herb renowned for its positive influence on dreams, giving protection, health, wealth and deepening one's psychic connection. Used in modern traditions for healing or common cold, stomach aches and anti-bacterial properties.

Frankincense—One of the most common herbs for incense and connecting in meditation to induce positive vibrations, and heightened levels of awareness. A balance between the fire and air elements this herb is a beautiful tool in cleansing, protection and spellcraft of raising vibrations.

Rosemary—The herb of memory, honor throughout time for its abilities to bring clarity and connection to the intellectual realms. Used by Wiccans for warding off evil, nightmares and giving protection, aiding in past life recall or even an aphrodisiac. This is favorite for the kitchen witch, for its diversity in the craft.

St. John's Wort—When in need of banishing spells, protection and cutting off the dark arts, this is the herb to call upon. Honored throughout the centuries for its protective and cleansing properties. Also used in divination, connecting with animals, power of positivity spells, good luck and success or merely commanding confidence.

Basil—Called upon for drawing wealth and abundance into life. Also used in love spells, protection, and healing. This is a powerful common herb to call into one's practice for many different areas.

Sage – The most common know use of sage in New Age spirituality is for smudging and cleansing practices. Sage has been revered by many ancient cultures for its cleansing use to ward of negative energies from people, places and objects. Even science is finding that the smoke kills bad bacteria in the air and purifies the oxygen we breathe, thus lifting our vibration.

The magical properties for herbs are nearly endless and one can does not wish to completely understand this magical realm within one lifetime alone. In my book *Wiccan Herbalism, a Beginners Grimoire*, we begin to explore in-depth the ways in which one can incorporate the magical properties into one's own practice. Exploring various magical baths and teas, to exploring the secrets of herbs themselves like lavender, frankincense, wormwood and more. Even diving into the history of herbalism, discovering the ways to create your own magical garden and learning how to conjure spells of abundance and protection through the secret powers that lay within the herbal kingdom, within these pages we will also explore some of these methods, yet for a more in-depth exploration of the herbal realms this can be a beautiful point of initiation for a beginner Wiccan on the path.

Pentacle

The pentacle, contrary to popular stereotypes, is not a just a five-pointed star or pentagram. In fact, a pentacle is traditionally a talisman upon which a symbol or magical image is engraved. Many Wiccan traditions believe that the pentacle is the most powerful symbol of the ancients and ways of old. For the pentacle traverses many religions and cultures throughout the ages. Unfortunately, throughout the Dark Ages myths have stuck to this symbol as a symbol of darkness and a harbinger of dark magic itself. Yet in truth this is a powerful symbol of protection and connection to the natural order of life.

Typically, a pentacle tends to be a flat and disc-shaped in orientation and may be composed of one or many materials such as woods or metals, yet also can be simply drawn on paper or cloth discs. The idea that a pentacle must contain the five-pointed star, or pentagram, was inspired by *Rider-Waite-Smith's Tarot Deck,* and this has since commonly been used for the design of a pentacle. This representation with the pentagram is the representation of the five elements, with the lower-left being Earth, Air is the upper left point, Fire the lower right and Water represented by the upper right, with the Spirit being the fifth point pointing straight upward. However, it is not uncommon to also find a pentacle with other magical symbols such as a hexagram, or six-pointed star, in addition to the popular pentagram design.

As being the single most powerful tool by many Wiccans this talisman is an essential part of any Wiccan practice. Many witches will wear a pentacle necklace for protection or to increase their abilities. For it is said that a pentacle carved from wood is a link to the natural world with a direct link to nature itself, whilst a pentacle made from gold will grant mental clarity, wisdom and energy. Yet, if forged from silver, the wearer's link to the Moon, The Goddess and the Psychic realms are at their strongest. In addition to being worn as a talisman or amulet, many practitioners will also have a pentacle on their altar to enhance this purity of energy, to honor nature and protect their sacred space.

Even used within various rituals and ceremonies. Folklore and tradition have led to the belief that there is a form of protection that can only be offered from the pentacle. Hence it is common that anyone whom dabbles within spell works or the craft will cast open, protect or even close their circle using the pentacle. This powerful tool can even be used during the ceremony or ritual to control and command various forces which may harm or be seen as negative entities, such as spirits or demons. Wiccans and pagans have used the pentacle in craft as a tool for controlling the spiritual realm for centuries and within modern day practice.

Crystals and Gemstones

Since the ways of old crystals and gemstones have been revered for their magical properties throughout all traditions. This appreciation and respect for these talismans of the earth is even still present today in alternative healing. Yet what exactly is a crystal? This term is loosely used within Wiccan or Neopaganism to encompass an array of various minerals and gemstones, that aren't necessarily crystals by the definition, yet commonly accepted this way. Essentially any mineral that has a molecular structure comprised of various patterns that form a flat surface or intricate geometrical pattern is generally referred to as a crystal.

One can notice the subtle ways the energies of these crystals speak by simply looking closely at the various angles, curvatures and patterns that are present in different stones. Wiccans and witches alike understand the power that lies within crystal magic is inherently the same power that lies within all-natural phenomenon, such as the river that flows or the wind that blows. As all matter, both visible and invisible matter, is energy and through learning to this universal energy we can learn to work in alignment with this natural power. The is a silent language that evokes the mysteries of the infinite, creative and divine that lives within Gaia that we learn access by slowing down and connecting with these powerful tools.

Many Wiccan and pagan traditions use gemstones and crystals as amulets, talisman's, pendants and offerings for protection, healing and many more magical crafts. Like the world of herbs, the study of crystals is a lifelong journey, for the deeper one goes the more one begins to question the mysteries that live among this earth. We find evidence of these healing minerals tied into folklore as well, with crystals like the clear quartz being used for a "crystal ball" as the quartz is known to amplify our psychic powers. Or we may find reference to rose quartz for self-love compared to that of smokey quartz for positive thoughts and grounding, the quartz family of crystals has a large array of properties and forms that it may take. Wicca often calls upon other popular crystals like amethyst for ethereal guidance or even the powers of tourmaline to protect from negative influence. As we continue to explore the workings of spells and the craft, we will call upon some of the following crystals within our work, and these can be a great entry point into the magical realm of crystal healing:

Clear Quartz—An all-purpose crystal for positive energy, amplifying the intent of the wearer or other crystals. Often worn to enhance spiritual connectivity and promote enlightenment. Great for balancing, healing, energy and personal power

Rose Quartz—A gentle pink version of the clear quartz used to promote love, peace, happiness and aid intolerance or even forgiveness. With a nurturing energy it is often believed to attract relationships, either romantic or friendship, to boost self-love and confidence. Wiccan traditions sees this crystal as a symbol of love.

Selenite – With the shimmering beauty and mystery of the moon, this crystal is believed to evoke the goddess energy. Known to recharge energy whilst cleansing negative energy this crystal is believed to connect the user to their intuition and spiritual guides, serving as a bridge between the physical and spiritual realms. Often used in spellcraft to promote purity, bring forth honesty and heighten personal vibrations.

Amethyst—Most commonly purple in color amethyst is known for its connection to our intuition and psychic powers through the third eye. Worn by Wiccans to promote inner strength, sobriety, self-discipline, self-awareness and peace. It is believed to also cleanses one's aura thus allowing for growth both spiritually and mentally. This is a powerful crystal commonly used in spell work and ceremonies involving meditation or connections to the spiritual realm, to gain insight into one's true self.

Black Onyx – The stone of endings, this is a powerful tool for banishing spells and cleansing of old patterns. Black onyx, as per its name is a solid black crystal, that resembles tourmaline, yet smoother. It is believed within traditions to aid in releasing spells, be a tool for protection and warding off negativity. Throughout time this crystal has been called upon to boost emotional well-being and enhance one's spiritual strength or self-confidence.

Tourmaline— Often worn for emotional stability, similar to its smooth counterpart black tourmaline is a stone of protection from negative spirits, patterns and to break obsessions by cleansing the wearers aura. Many witches and empaths will carry this stone to protect from feeling the emotional states of others surrounding them, as it is said to dispel chaotic energy or scattered vibrations becoming a shield against inner and outer harm or psychic attack. This is a powerful magical tool for any Wiccan wishing for a calm and balanced state of mind in all moments.

Tigers Eye— The gentle browns and golden stripes of a tigers eye often form the pattern that come to an eye shape at the center of the crystal and have a very grounding essence merely by seeing the stone. Worn to deter illusion, give clear perception and reveal the truth of a situation tigers eye is said to give the wearer the ability to detect manipulation, or dishonest intent. Often associated with luck and protection this is also a crystal used in the craft for willpower, loyalty, integrity and courage whilst also keeping one grounded throughout the spell work.

Moon Stone—This gently milky grey crystal as a stone representing the goddess and moon energies. Revered for its magical properties that bring clarity to intuition, life cycles, deep connections with people and empathy. Wicca often calls in the moonstone for divination and clairvoyant rituals or ceremonies. Known to bring kindness to the wearer, it is common to find a witch with a moonstone close to their heart.

Jasper—Similar to the quartz family there is many variations of jasper, yet it can be identified by its earthy organic veins that are usually present in the crystal. Sometimes referred to as a "hard-working stone" jasper is known to aid in careers or business ventures to clear the way for steadfast work. Used in the craft for spells to bring organization, diligence, balance, perseverance or even assertiveness it is truly a grounding stone for the Wiccan whom is ingrained in the modern pace of life.

Of course, these are just a handful of magical crystals and gemstones that one can begin to work with throughout their spell workings. Take the time to explore, observe and experience the various properties that crystals have you and your practice. Each Wiccan will have different experiences with these stones, so honor those that resonate to your own essence, and notice how these changes over time as your vibration also changes.

With this handful of magical tools, we are ready to continue our exploration into magical realms of Wicca. Know that as we continue each tradition calls upon its own version of these magical tools and as you progress down the path your own grimoire will continue to expand, and knowledge of these ancient tools will unfold as needed. Also have the open mind though, that it is not essential to have a large array of tools, for they are only tools and one can still practice forms of magic and elements of the craft without tools, just by connecting to their intent.

Chapter 3: Sacred Space Altars and Circles

Creating a sacred space for your craft is an important process of any Wiccan practice. Each tradition has its own methods of how to cultivate these spaces, some have more than one. First you may wish to look to your tradition to the learn the ways in your own lineage. However, if you are a solitary witch or merely looking to cultivate your own method of sacred spaces let us look into some traditional methods of holding space. For our sacred space is the place where the majority of our craft takes place, perhaps we use an altar for worship or even ceremonial spells, or we may cast a circle to purify the energy for our spell work or even both ways may be called upon for different practices within the craft. If these terms do not make sense to you yet, do not worry for in the coming pages we will explore how to set your own altar, how to cast a circle and what these both mean. To provide you the wisdom, knowledge and confidence to truly create your own sacred space to move forward within the craft!

Purpose of Altars

A Wiccan altar is defined as a "raised place or structure used for worship or prayer." Within many sacred traditions, religions and cultures the altar is often the focal point for rituals and ceremonies, as is the way within the Wiccan rite. Each tradition and ceremony may call for various forms of the altar or use the altar for differing purposes, however it is essentially a table or space used for holding rituals tools, symbols for giving offerings and is also seen as a workspace for spell casting. An altar can be set up anywhere that a Witch has the space, keeping in mind that this is the focal point of your spell work and ritual, meaning it is a sacred magical space.

Often referred to as the heart of a sacred space, the altar is the seat of worship. Thus many religions or even individual practitioners will always hold a sacred space between their altar and the general public, only allowing the chosen to engage in altering of the altar, this may be the high priest or priestess, or religious leader of a group, a solitary witch may have their altar only in their bedroom or sacred space, away from the eyes of guests. For within Wicca this is a place of private communion between yourself, your Gods and the celebrating the sacred divine. Thus, this is in many traditions a very personal space, not for the entire community to experience. Within circles there is often a temporary altar set and consecrated for the ceremony that is for all those present, yet often, you would find this is not the primary altar.

There are many types of altars within various traditions for different purposes. Traditional altars may also resemble a shrine, which is essentially a space for veneration. This form of altar may be set permanently at your home or in your sacred space, this form of altar is often used to honor a particular spirit, deity or household guardian. These traditional altars are a great space for prayers or meditation to connect with this energy. These altars are often rather basic and need not be elaborate, yet many witches alter these shrines for more elaborate ceremonies like Samhain Season's or at certain stages of the Wheel of Life. We will explore shortly various ways to set this type of altar within your own craft. Another form may be a temporary altar, similarly for various ceremonies or rituals. This type of altar can simply be added to a fixed altar in your home or even be a "portable altar", this type of altar is referred to as a *Ritual Altar*. A ritual altar for a ceremony such as Samhain for example may then be set up in a different room from your shrine. Allowing this to also be a more public altar for anyone who may enter your home or space during this seasonal time. Thus, giving honoring not only the spirits but also this time within the Wheel of Life. Yet another form of altar is referred to as the *Working Altar*. As per its name this form of altar is often used for specific spell work or rituals. With a working altar at times you may only need this setup for a evening practice or Esbat ceremony, yet it is also not uncommon for spells to call upon an altar dedicated to the spell for a longer duration of time. When using altars for spell work it is important that they are not cluttered with any decorations, tools or energies that are not specifically used for this spell, making these altars often the most simplistic yet still just as powerful. Whilst all three of these altars may require space to be set, and we will explore shortly how to set your own altar, there is yet also many Wiccan traditions also utilize portable altars or a *Box Shrine*. These forms are often smaller and perfect for the traveling solitary Wiccan. Similar to the above styles a box shrine may be dedicated to just one deity, with objects honoring this deity, or even with various magical tools that may be used within the craft. This is a magical way to still hold a sacred space, with limited room or space, or whilst on the road. It is common and perfectly fine to have one altar for more than one purpose, or even have multiple styles of altars throughout your home. You may have an altar in the kitchen dedicated Hestia whilst a shrine set in the garden for Dionysus with then a third in ritual altar in another room dedicated to Sabbat or Esbat ceremonies. Remember this is an expression of your connection to the divine, making an altar(s) that is personal to you is the key. Take the time to first distinguish the intent of the altar will help you plan where to set it and also which tools are going to best serve the function of your altar. Let us explore some ways to set this sacred space for your future magical endeavors.

How to set an altar

Setting your first altar may seem like a daunting task at first, however it is actually rather exciting and a magical way of connecting to the divine, even sometimes overexciting that we know not where to begin. As we have seen there are many forms of altars so first knowing the intent for our sacred space will assist in giving us some direction. Knowing whether you will be using this as a shrine and worship or exploring the workings of rituals and spell casting or possibly your own practices like chanting, meditation, prayer or even more. This is your space and your connection to the sacred. First set this intent and then we can easily go from here.

There are a few commonalities between most altars, such as being a raised surface like a table, desks, shelves or even a stump in nature. Additionally, to the physical surface, one would often cover this surface with a chosen cloth before laying down some traditional items. Whilst of course there are specific altar adornments there is also some more commonly found tools that are generally within Wiccan or pagan tradition, note these are by no means mandatory, as every altar is unique, but may include:

- Athame- A ceremonial knife or blade, used in the Wiccan tradition. Often
- Broom
- Candle(s)

- Cauldron
- Chalice
- Incense
- Pentacle
- Wand

As you begin this assembly of tools and formation of your sacred space, look to various traditions to see why they call upon certain tools and their purpose. Your altar should be set to reflect the characteristics, personality, aesthetic, interests and intent of you as the creator. Through the combination of these traditional components and other optional components take the time to customize and assemble the right magical components for your altar, also knowing this can, and most likely will, be rearranged over time as your intent changes. This is a sacred space for you to feel relaxed, connected and invigorated all at once as soon as you connect with this space. Thus, adding some additional ornaments of tools of the craft can also deepen your connection, and be a great way to honor various Esbats, Sabbats, Deities or the current season. A few common extras that can be found may include:

- Live plants
- Crystals, Rocks or Minerals
- Dried Flowers, Herbs and Plants

- Jewelry
- Animal Remains
- Crafts, Drawings or Writings
- Anything else you feel drawn to add

Let us undertake the journey together that may unfold as we create our own first altar step by step. From here you will have the knowledge to confidently make your own sacred space;

Step One- Once your intent is known for your sacred space choosing the appropriate surface or base is a key component. Often Wiccans will use a table or a shelf, yet theoretically if you have a flat surface to place your tools of the craft upon you have the perfect surface. Size of this surface is important as this space must be spacious enough to accommodate each item and any additional items you may wish to add. Wiccans may use tables, such as a small coffee table or desk can be perfect, keeping in mind height will play an aspect in your rituals; for example, will you be kneeling, sitting or standing when connecting to your altar. Folklore also says that tables that are more weathered, or aged hold more character, than a newly purchased table. Another way you could upcycle your altar is by converting an old milk crate, dresser draw or another sturdy item of furniture that is no longer needed for its original purpose, if you take this option be sure to cleanse your old furniture and cover with a cloth to charge it with new energy. As Wicca and Paganism is about cultivating a connection to nature tradition has often seen a tree stump used as an altar setting, that also still holds that natural look and energy. Of course, these are just some recommendations and any other creative ideas will also serve.

Step Two- Location, location, location. The setting and directional orientation of your sacred altar are extremely important for the heart of your sacred space. This is of course a matter of personal choice and convenience as to how you can set your altar. However, considering indoor or outdoor settings can change the intent of your altar. Traditionally outdoor altars have been common for those who commune frequently with nature and the elements, this may mean frequently assembling or disassembling your altar throughout the Wheel of Life. For this reason, many Wiccans decide on a permanent altar set indoors, with the addition of a small portable altar for outdoor ceremonies, like that of a box altar.

Here directional orientation is also a point to consider, although not necessary. Many Wiccans will choose to set their altar to a particular cardinal direction either to align with the Northern point like a pentacle or possible to the direction of the rising or setting Sun/ Moon to honor this time. Additionally, the honoring of which elements most correspond within your tradition, one may set their altar to face the direction corresponding with this elemental energy – North for water, East for air, South with fire, and west to honor earth.

Step Three- Once the altar has a location, a surface now we must adorn it with the traditional magical tools or symbols of offering. As mentioned above there is a list of various common and optional magical tools found on a Wiccan altar. Wiccan altars will often have an offering to each of the four physical elements, with either a pentacle or a small offering to each element in each of the four cardinal points. One may offer a small bowl of sand or dirt for the earth, a candle or charcoal for fire, incense can be representative of air, and a small bowl of water as the final offering. The athame is a key magical tool for most rituals so placing one on your altar can charge it with the energy of your altar and is recommended for the use through ceremony. As a wand is used to direct energy this can be a good addition to your altar, if you use one. A candle can also be placed on the altar as an offering to the Goddess or cultivating a certain intention through the color of the candle. Some Wiccans will even keep their Book of Shadows on their altar to keep it within pure energy and always at hand. The placement of these magical tools is up to you and what resonates most clearly with the intent of your altar.

Step Four- Once you have adorned your altar with the traditional magical tools, taking the time to add and decorate your space with optional extras can be a beautiful way to personify your altar. These items are what will make the space your own unique channel to the divine, truly aligning it with the goals of your practice and creating it such a way that you enjoy spending time at your altar each day. As briefly explored, this may include the addition of crystals, minerals, plants, herbs, jewelry, arts, crafts, writings, animal remains or the likes. The main intentions of this step is so you may;

- Wish to spend more time at your altar each day;
- Be reminded of your goals and focus of the craft;
- That it holds significance and meaning to your life;
- It makes you altar feel unique and authentic to your vision;
- Also, that it may direct your energy and focus each day.

Just to keep in mind that this is a sacred space, so also being created with clarity and pure intent is an element to consider avoiding being a cluttered space. Throughout times you may add additional offerings like cakes, teas, ale and more to your altar at times of Esbat or Sabbat or even decorating for the seasonal celebrations. Regardless of how you construct your altar, be sure it contains all your magical tools you may need for an effective ritual *before* beginning your ceremony or magical workings.

Step Five- Placement can also be a part of the magic when bringing your altar together. This is something to explore of time, what happens when you change the placement of your magical tools and noting the difference it makes to the energy that flows through this space. Once you have figured out the ways in which to best set your altar and the placement of each item, sketching or photographing the space in your Book of Shadows can also be beneficial so you may recreate this space if need be. As you practice various spell work or rituals you may also change the orientation of you altar accordingly such as the follow suggestions, always remember this is your space these are only suggestions to help you along the way;

An altar for deities:

- If you honor only a singular deity, one would often place a statue, image or feature offering at the center or just behind the center point of the altar. With a candle either side and all other tools around it.
- To give respects to the God and the Goddess, the symbol for the God usually sits to the right whilst the offering for the Goddess goes to the left.

- However, for multiple deities aligning the various representation of symbols along the back of the altar in a straight line.

Altar for the Elements:

- Place the symbols for each element on the front and center of the altar aligning them with quarters if desired, this will allow for convenient handling in ceremony.
- Alternatively, place the representations at the four corners of the altar aligning their corresponding quarters to their cardinal points.
- Water and Earth can sit to the left side of the Goddess, as they represent the divine feminine; whilst the Fire and Air will go to the right side of the altar to represent the masculine energy points.

Traditional Wiccan Tools

- Place these tools are the front and center can be useful on working altars, align them in various quarters accordingly with your tradition.
- Commonly the chalice and pentacle are placed to the left as they are feminine symbols, whilst the

athame and wand typically go to the right side as expressions of the masculine symbols.

- Alternatively, for a ritual table place your pentacle at the center, lay your wand and athame across the corners or edge of the table for during the ceremony and finally the chalice to the left side of the altar.

Again, these are all just guidelines for you to find your own unique expression. Explore the placements, ornaments and altars that most honor your practice, keeping in mind you need not be limited to only one style or one altar either. Notice and accept that your altar will change over time within your development of the craft, this is perfectly ok and often encouraged by many traditions. Enjoy the process and may this serve as a guide for you to begin with creating your own sacred space.

Circles

Throughout many esoteric traditions and cultures circles have always been a symbol of mysticism and used for various spiritual rituals, ceremonies or create sacred space, the circle has become a foundation of the Wiccan traditions. Whilst some various religions or traditions may have churches, temples or mosques as their sacred space "the casting of the circle", or sometimes referred to as "Erecting the Temple Rite," is seen as the equivalent rite in Wicca lore. This is due to the belief that the circle serves as a protective barrier or even as a force field creating a container for the caster to be protected from the magical forces they are working with. Wiccan groups are often not large enough in size to call for erect buildings to gather in and often rituals take place within nature, making the Circle the perfect portable sacred space. Some covens believe that it is the perfect symbol to represent the evermoving, constantly transforming energy of the Wiccan way, that which has no beginning nor an end. With the common belief throughout the craft that one's spirituality is an energy and belief to carry with you no matter where you go.

The casting of a circle itself is in fact a 2-dimensional symbol for what is in fact a sphere. As many Wiccans understand the circle itself is merely the area where the energetic sphere connects with the ground. For when we cast a circle, we are erecting a spherical temple that also creates a bubble above and below the earth, protecting from the sky and the core of the earth. Thus, this energetic vortex contains the energy of your spell work into a condensed space allowing the energy to be supercharged, in a sense, and then fully released at the end of the spell to increase the potency of your intent and manifestation from your workings.

Within the Wiccan tradition the circle was adopted from Ceremonial Magic. This form of magic heralds from what is referred to as Abrahamic Worldview, the belief that angels, demons and spirits are energies forms that are summoned to be controlled. Yet within the Wiccan tradition, this view is often not common belief; as it is merely not the purpose of Wiccan rituals. Rather the Wiccan way uses the Circle for the containing and charging of energy, but also for keeping the negative energy or debris out from our spell work. This way we create a sacred space for containing the positive vibrations and energies that are conjured during our spell work and keep the practitioner, spirits and deities that may be called upon during our ritual clear, pure and worshipped by only pure vibration.

Some traditions debate whether the casting of a Circle is completely necessary whilst others believe it is without a doubt. This obviously comes down to the caster and coven, however there are many reasons as to how this can be an extremely beneficial practice. For as is the way in all Wiccan tradition, there is no one right or wrong way. Yet when cast correctly the circle will become a great assistance to your spiritual growth and practice along the Wiccan path. As it also promotes a sense of tradition or ritual of its own, connecting one to the Wiccan rite and ways of old. Giving the practice a fluid, complete and whole formation. It is believed to also give a witch a sense of how to direct, manipulate and sense energy whilst also creating a space to come into communication with deities, spirits or the elements from a pure heart.

Many Wiccans will always cast a permeant circle around their altar or within their home to honor this sacred space.

Additionally, they will make regular practice of casting a circle before any spell work and closing it after the practice to also release the energy again. The more regularly an initiate practice the more attuned one can become to the powers of casting a circle, some witches are known to even just cast a circle to sit in for meditation or merely to experience the vibrations this can contain. One does not need to be initiated into a special way of circle casting or be a High Priestess/Priest, anyone can begin to cast circles, even if they are not a Wiccan. With this in mind it is strongly encouraged for any Wiccan to learn how to cast a circle and continuing practicing to master this art.

How to cast a Circle:

The casting of a circle is something that often takes time, patience and of course practice. So, do not be discouraged at first if you do not connect with your circle, this will come in time, practice is key. Many traditions have their own rituals or ways of casting circle, and you may be able to connect with a local Wiccan to guide you through the art, alternatively we can explore a few tips, guidelines and even a 'ritual script' below to start you along the path. Keeping in mind that as this is your circle this will only serve as a framework for your own casting rituals, and give inspiration however it is important as you progress that you develop, edit and adjust the practices to those that most resonate with your craft.

The understanding of energy is a key component to casting your circle. This means that tools like meditation, visualization and energy play are going to serve you in preparation for not only your circle casting, yet all spell work as you continue down the path. Let us take moment to explore these three tools before we continue, and I encourage you to continuously come back to cultivating these tools, not only for casting circles, yet in all of your magical workings. For as you will surely discover as you continue down the path the understanding of energy, meditation and visualization are the foundational aspects of any magical work, hence we find that at the base of most spiritual religions and practices since the ancient times.

Meditation

Meditation is going to be your first step, as is the way for most practices on the spiritual path and understanding of the spiritual realms. Mastering meditation will serve as a guide to anyone wishing to dive into understanding and connecting with energy. There are of course many techniques and versions of meditation, yet for the understanding of energy and connecting to the spiritual realm, focusing on your breath, mind and relaxation will guide you along the way. Simply take the time to sit and focus on your breath. In theory this sounds simple enough yet anyone whom has experienced these states understands this too also takes practice. Again, there are many forms you can explore to dive into the realms of meditation and connect to this meditative state.

Through basic breathing exercises however you will learn how to calm the mind and slip into these meditative states at will. Take the time to find a comfortable, stable seat and gently close your eyes. It can help to be in a quiet calm space, and to also be sitting upright is key, otherwise we tend to fall asleep at first. Once you are in this stable space and eyes closed, merely focus on your breath. Just noticing the inhalation and exhalation. Notice the way it feels, tastes and smells, even bring your attention to the sound it makes coming in and out. Each time you realize the mind is wandering off or thinking of something else, and it will, gently bring your attention back to your breath. Focusing on the in and out of each breath. Allow yourself the time to sit and practice this even for 5-10 minutes daily and you will begin to notice how the mind begins to slow down its thoughts a little more each day. This will allow you to begin noticing the energy that is moving in and around your body just through your breath and ultimately serve as a foundation for the spell work, we will continue to explore and cultivate.

Visualization

Throughout the craft one is often connecting to the spiritual realms, or other energies that are commonly invisible to the human eye. Thus, we must learn to cultivate what is called the inner vision or as the Indian Yogi's would call it our Third eye. Visualization is a core ability in any ritual work for that which you cannot imagine one cannot manifest. Now as we investigate tools for visualization it is also important to note that this may come through variety of sense, as some people will be able to see colors, shapes, energies or objects whilst other people will more have a feeling or sensation of sounds, smells, tastes and emotions as their inner visualization. Hence this is another area to be mastered over time and as you practice it is encouraged not only to focus on one sensory outlet but all of them, bringing the sights, sounds, smells, tastes and feelings- both emotional and physical. This will ultimately increase the accuracy and potency of your intent in you spell work as you progress.

A visualization exercise you may work with may be as broad as meditation techniques, however essentially you want to enter a meditative state and then call in these various techniques. One great way to practice is through the visualization of colors associated with a number or point of the body. For example, in this state with your eyes closed picture a Red 1 within your third eye, placing this red 1 at the base of your spine. Once you have this vision, next imagine an Orange 2 this time placing it at your belly button. Take the time to really envision these colors and numbers, finally slowly picturing the placement on the body. Then continue to work your way up. With a Yellow 3 on your solar plexus, a Green 4 at your heart center, followed by a Blue 5 at your throat, then 6 is Indigo in between your eyebrows and finally a Violet 7 on the crown of your head. These numbers and colors also are the alignment of the Chakras, wheels of energy, that flow along you body, thus working not only on your visualization but also aligning the flow of energy in your system preparing your body and mind for further magic work to come. If at first you are struggling to envision these colored numbers of points of the body, simply draw a Violet 7 on a piece of paper, stare it for some time then picture it within your third eye. This will help create and connect to your inner vision over time.

As you learn to connect with this visualization exercise more quickly and fluidly you can even begin to expand on these exercises becoming more complexed in your visualization. You may even begin to recall various places from childhood. Picking a family home and recalling the different colors, sounds, smells or feelings of this place. These exercises will continue to strengthen your inner sight which you will need in more complex spell working and even for the casting of a perfect circle. By continuing to practice this for even 5 minutes a day you will find you are quickly able to call upon this inner sight to deepen your connection to the spiritual realms.

Energy Flow

Now that you have a connection to your meditative state and inner sight one can begin to focus on the flow of energy. As it is important when casting an effective circle that we can manipulate the flow of energy. This will allow us to be a channel for which energies serve the ritual and are needed within the circle and which are best to be protected against to be able to cast the most effective spells or keep a pure sacred space for rituals and ceremonies. Energy is drawn not only from the casting with but also from the collective surroundings, so you will also be drawing energy in from the universe itself, celestial realms, the elements and all forms of Gaia.

This practice of connecting to the flow of energy is also where you will need to call upon your visualization to be able to see beyond your 2-dimensional circle and create the spherical energy. When first practice it can help to simply sit in a meditative state and work with your own energy. Traditions often teach this by placing your palms a few inches away from one another not quite touching and then take the time to sense your own energy, you may wish to push and pull yours hands closer and further away to notice the energy that flows. Many people often did this as children not realizing that we are in fact playing with the subtler energies of the cosmos. Once you have become familiar with your own energy play with that of other people's energy, trying the same method with a friend's hand. This will allow you to realize what is your energy compared to that of someone else, a valuable lesson to learn when considering energy working like magic.

After time you may wish to take this energy flow one step further and begin to play with the manipulation of the flow. This is easily practiced by being in a dimly lit room. Once you have learnt recognize your own energy, then you can begin to see it also, simply by repeating the above exercise yet this time staring at your hands you may begin to see the aura or subtle body around your hands. Again, do not be disheartened if this takes time to practice or if you cannot see anything, some people will be able to feel rather than see, honor your process. Once you can either see, feel or sense this energy start to play with expanding and contracting it. Visualize yourself casting this energy around your body or at another object and notice what arises. Notice how this changes the energy around you or within you. This is what is meant by energy manipulation and this is one of the first steps to casting your circle and diving into the realms of Wiccan magic.

Circle Casting

The ritual of casting a circle has many forms and techniques. One may simply call upon the circle energetically, one may perform an entire ritual or as mentioned some have this a set sacred space. This is entirely up to you to connect uniquely with your practice. Yet patience and practice are the key to mastering the art of circle casting. As you learn this craft you can easily cast a circle anywhere and at any moment. Whether this be for rituals, spell work or to simply sit in for meditation at night in your own room. So, let us explore various forms of circle casting.

One method may be simply an energetic circle, using your powers of visualization take the time to connect to a meditative state to envision the energy building in-side your own body. Visualizing the energy flowing up from the Earth itself into your center and the energy flowing down from the universe above you. Allow these energies to harmonize within you and transform as they connect with your own energy. From here allow this energy to form a sphere or bubble inside of you. Focusing your intent on this bubble watch as it begins to grow and expand from within you to outside of you until you are surrounded by this bubble. This is a perfect way to practice this energy manipulation and cast a circle around yourself for rituals or meditation.

Alternatively, you may wish to set a physical circle to perform your rituals or ceremonies or simply honor your altar. This will also work with the above visualization as it is still important to set your intent, for any form of spellcrafts, including circle casting. Here is a ritual to cast your circle and some of the materials you may need;

Magical tools:

Cord, Stones, Candles, Crystal, Sand, Salt, Chalk or Copper Wire (optional)

Smudge Stick (sage) or Palo Santo

Wand, Power Finger or Athame

Any further materials you need to perform the ritual or spell work.

Step One- Cleanse and Prepare Space (Use this technique for all spell work that calls for smudging)

This is always recommended to purify the space in preparation for the coming works.

- Using your cord, candles, crystal, sand, salt, copper or item of choice, outline the edge of your circle. Folklore would call for a circle of 9 feet in diameter, as this is sacred numerology, however you can cast to your own sizing. The main factor is that you and your ritual items fit within the space with ease. *This is an optional step to assist manifesting the circle, yet you can just energetically call upon this space.*
- Cleanse the four directions. Light your smudge stick directing it to the East of your circle. Drawing a line

straight up and down with the incantation "I cleanse the space to the East."

- Next cleansing the South, moving in this direction draw a line straight up and down with the spell "I cleanse the space to the South".

- Continue this pattern to the West and then the North. Each time stepping in the direction you wish to cleanse drawing this line with your smudge stick and repeating the incantation with its direction.

- Finally cleanse the center of this space to represent the element of the Spirit, walking close-wise in the circle take a spiral formation so you end up in the center of the circle. Repeating "I cleanse the space in between.

- Once you arrive at the center remain here and cleanse yourself, including under your feet, in between your hands and around your head. The chant "I cleanse myself" is said at this time.

- Finally finish the cleansing by putting out the smudge stick and stating, "Myself and the space are clear and cleansed with purity."

-

Step Two- Calling your Circle into being.

This will cast a sphere of positive energy around your being, sealing your circle with pure universal energy. Be sure to have everything you need for your magical works with you before calling this circle.

Draw Down the Energy.

- Standing at the center of your circle, turn to be facing the East. From here point your wand or power hand to the point where the edge of the circle and earth meet one another.
- With your opposing index finger pointed towards the sky, calling upon the Universe. Visualize a white light, a violet light or your own power color from your tradition, coming down from the universe. Feel this light coursing through your body and from one hand to the other hand. See the light projecting from your wand and traveling from the ground.

Cast the Circle.

- Turning clockwise, visualizing that you are drawing a line of white or pure ultraviolet light around the perimeter of your circle. See this create a glowing flame or light casting a line to draw your circle. Continue turning clockwise until you have come to face the East again. Allowing your circle to overlap and closing on itself. Your circle will be cast. From here you are ready to claim this space as your own.

Claim your Space.

- Remain standing in the center of your magical circle, raise your hands high and say:

"This is a time; that is not a time, in a place that is not a place.
Here I stand at the threshold, between the worlds, before the mystery of the veil.
Here may the Ancient one's manifest. Here may they bless their child."

You have now finished creating and casting your magical circle. From here complete your magical workings connecting with this pure magical energy allowing for the amplifying of your intent and spellcraft to come to life. This is also the space in which you can call upon for personal deities, guides or spirits to connect and help you with your magical workings. Note this connection may take time to cultivate an is often recommended for the Adept or Advanced practitioner to harness. Once you finish your spell workings closing the circle is the final stage of any circle, to bring the practice full circle.

Release Your Circle

This will allow you to send the energy cultivated within your circle and practice out into the universe to become manifest.

Bind the energy of your spell

-Once finished the workings, come to the center of your circle or stand by your altar. Raising your hands or wand to the sky, call to the universe "Now, I bind all the power within this circle into this spell, so mote it Be."

Release the Spirits or Entities

-If you called upon any deities, entities or spirits in your practice take this time to thank them for their assistance and allow them to be released.

Pull up the Energy

-Turn to face the East. Point your wand or recessive hand to face the boundary of your circle and its connection to the Earth. Guide your dominant hand to the sky with the index finger pointing to the center of the universe. Visualize this circle being drawn back into your recessive hand, traveling down and through your body, and channel this energy back up into the universe through your dominant hand.

Release Your Circle

-Turning counterclockwise in your circle begin imagining/ visualizing the energy flowing back up into the sky manifesting your spell work. Continue your circle thrice until you return to face the East again. Know and feel that your magical intent has now been sent out into universe to be manifest into reality, allowing the universe to work with this magic. Your circle is now completely released.

Close Your Sacred Space

-From the center point of your circle, bring your hands to the heavens and call out "The circle is now closed, yet it always remains a circle. Around and through me may this magical flow of power be."

Now you have the tools to begin casting your own circles. Whether this be through visualization and energetic flow or through the ritual and connection to magical tools, take the time to practice and notice the power of your circles grow. As you continue to practice notice which elements you can refine, which elements are the strongest in your own manifestation of energy.

Over time this will guide you to greater spellcrafting and serve as a guide for the beginning of your witchcraft. You may find other rituals or incantations along your path that more honor your unique gifts, honor these truths. This is simply a guide to help you along the path to understanding the magical power of circle magic. Now we can continue to cultivate our magical workings and explore the secrets of spellcraft to align with our sacred spaces.

Chapter 4 The Realm of Spells

Before we continue into our list of spells and creating our own grimoire of the craft, let us develop an understanding of various forms of magic we may encounter. Through this understanding we will allow the opportunity to be more equip in the knowledge and wisdom to truly cultivate magic in our lives and practice. Within all realms of magic and spellcraft it is important to understand patience and persistence are key virtues. For it is through these virtues that we can connect with our greatest potential, otherwise we may miss the subtlest layers of magic and ways in which our spellcraft is working or can even be improved in time. Once we have an understanding of these types of magic, methods of improving and also acknowledging the subtly and complexity of magic then you will be truly be ready to be an accomplished spellcaster of the Wiccan way.

What are different spells for different purposes?

Often as we begin along the Wiccan path and dive into the world of spell casting it can seem overwhelming at first. As we find that there is not merely one spell for abundance, or one spell to cultivate luck, rather we are faced with an array of options. This is because as we are cultivating magic one of foundational components is the intent, and this intent, in many cases, needs to be very specific. Thus, throughout the centuries and traditions many spells have been adapted and modified to really narrow down the intent of that spell. A key to remember here is that these spells are only a guide along the path. The wisdom from those who have walked the path before us, yet there is nothing wrong at all with using these spells or even cultivating your own spells. Both paths will serve the Wiccan tradition and bring magic into life. So, if you feel overwhelmed at first, do not fear, in time you will learn how to navigate your own way through the sea of spells, to truly cultivate those that are most beneficial for you. Eventually, you will even learn how to modify and develop your own spells that align with your craft. For now, we have begun to understand the history of magic, explored some of the forms it can take now let us begin seeing how to cultivate this intent through the workings of spell casting.

Inner and Outer Magic

We will find in this world of magic various forms of spells. Many Wiccans will encompass the world of spells into two major categories, one being the world of inner magic whilst the other is the realms of outer magic. The world of inner magic works with spells of introspection, the more intimate workings, moving through the subconscious and often working with meditation, affirmations and mantras. The intent with this category is often about creating a sacred space internally to make space for personal intimacy and revelation, allowing the access through your subconscious. Witch's may call upon this spellcraft for introspective work with the intention as simple as recall to find a lost object or as intricate and complex as fixing a relationship problem. Outer magic is often about connecting to the Higher Being, through humbling devotional work connecting with prayers, invocations and devotional rituals. This means as we move forward to reach out our connection to an external force. We surrender to a Higher Energy being in control through this form of magic. Some think of this as a form of prayer, as it adopts an attitude of humility, devotion and acceptance. This form of spell casting can often take consistent practice to surrender more and more deeply, or even work with magical devotional tools.

Wealth vs Abundance Spells

Once we have understood the concept of Inner and Outer magic, we find there is even subtler layers of spellcraft. For as we explore the realm of spellcraft, we discover basic forms of good luck spells, attracting abundance onto your threefold is a common belief in Wiccan good luck spells. Or we may work more with spells of wealth and money, as this can be more specific than just overall abundance. Whereas abundance may also bring abundance in health, wealth and love, we can narrow down our intent and focus on drawing solely financial abundance through wealth and money spells. Wealth and money spells may work on an inner level, changing our belief, goals or expectations around money thus opening our subconscious and vibrational energy to the flow of money into our lives. These can be a great tool for grounding and opening more possibilities within life. We will explore these in more depth in the coming pages.

Love, Binding & Banishing Spells

We may even work with love spells to attract, receive or give more love within your life. Love spells are a form of spellcasting that requires extremely precise clarity to truly draw the correct intent into your life. The most potent forms of love spells are those working on how much love one can give receive, by opening our inner landscape to receive more love we begin to see this attracted to us. Shortly we will dive into the realms of love spells with more depth and understanding as these can actually be the trickiest spells to understand. However, once we have an in-depth grasping of this magic, we can attract far more than just romantic love into our life with the same principles.

Whilst love spells are used for attracting and giving more love, sometimes we require spells for banishing or releasing old loves and patterns. This is where the Wiccan practitioner often turns to banishing spells or clearing spells. As per its name this spell works of repelling, banishing or clearing energies rather attracting them as we see in love spells. Wiccans often call upon these spells to clear curses, protect from spirits or cleanse past relationships, to name a few uses for this powerful magical tool.

Both forms of spells, whilst seemingly opposites can actually be used to assist one another and enhance the intent of the caster. For the banishing or clearing spells may even be used to clear our energy of an old lover, friend or relationship that is ultimately stopping us from drawing in a new love to our life.

Traditional and Folklore magic

As we have now seen Wicca is deeply rooted in traditions, folklore and ancient wisdom. Whilst this is important to our craft, do not allow this to overwhelm you, in time this understanding will develop and build. For there are literally eons of knowledge, that one cannot wish to learn in one lifetime of practice. Over time what is relevant will come and build this understanding. You will often find small side notes in spells, that give hints to why we cast in certain ways and this can be the most beneficial way of understanding this tradition magic. For example, some folklore and particularly the lore of Native America tradition, spells are sealed within a jar, bottle or a form of container. This is with the belief that the jar will contain the potency of the spell and prevents the magic from depleting before the spell is complete. Whilst some spells are based around the opposite belief of releasing the magic into the universe with practices like candle magic and releasing the alchemical magic into the universe as the candle burns, or the ways of chanting and incantation to allow the vocal energy to be sent out into the cosmos. These ways are merely a reflection of the two overarching categories of spell work, the realms of the inner magic and outer magic. We find these subtler techniques however can be used for both attracting or repelling our intent. So, our main tool within all spell work be not the device or physical tools yet our intent and ways of cultivating the magic. Hence, the importance on meditation, visualizations and cultivating sacred spaces so we may hold this sacred intent in perfect trust clarity and love. From here we can continue to strengthen this intent with our tools of spell work.

But are my spells working?

Spell casting can be also a practice of patience, as we may not always see the results instantly. Yet allow for space and time after your spell casting before jumping to conclusions. Remember spell casting and magic is a sacred art form, it may take practice before your first spell harvests results. Many traditions will say to wait for 28 days, a full lunar cycle, before recasting your spell. It is also believed to truly understand the results of a spell we must not just keep recasting spells hoping for results yet casting one abundance spell and waiting before recasting is more powerful than 3-4 spells of abundance all at once. As this way we keep our intention clear and concise so the universe can pick up the message and respond, rather than multiple messages coming at once.

So how can we see if this magic is really working though? For many practitioners when they first step on the path doubt can be our biggest downfall, as this can lessen the magic response. However, to go beyond the doubt we also need the faith to know our magical workings are really working. When our magic begins to first at first the signs may be subtle before the fullest fruition of the spell comes into being. You may notice a change in your mood or emotions. If you cast a spell for new love, at first you may begin seeing the world with a new open heart. Noticing the way, the wind moves through the trees, the laughter of children or the smile people have all of a sudden brings you more joy, happiness and peace. You may begin to feel more cleansed, energized or bright throughout your day, for this is indicating a shift in your aura as more love and compassion are flowing into your being. These can be signs that you are beginning to open to love more and within time your new lover will be on their way. Continue to focus on these subtle changes in mood and emotions as this is the first sign that your magic is working. With this said however, do not feel disheartened if you are not seeing these emotions straight away, it may be the spell cleansing old patterns or showing you that you could have been more grounded during the spell. This can be a valuable lesson to receive in our spell casting.

Another indication that are spells are beginning to work is that the universe is starting to call to you. Wicca often calls these signs from the universe Omens. These omens are often nature or animals starting to connect with you as a guide that your spellcraft is working. The Indigenous tribes of Australia have been known to look to these omens in nature to indicate the ways magic is working, the same was the way for the Celts of old or Native American traditions, and Wicca has adopted this into their beliefs. It is believed that cloud formations, patterns in the trees or even flocks of birds can be seen as omens to tell us to keep going. Take the time to reflect after you spell work in nature, look and listen to the natural world around you as signs are often subtle yet powerful for the craft.

Dreams are a great teacher. A Wiccan knows that all dreams have purpose and meaning to. Pay attention to the wisdom in the dreams, these can be a way to notice the workings of our magic. This can be our intuition or Higher Self communicating to us through our unconscious mind. If you have cast a spell for abundance or receiving more money, you may begin to dream of receiving a new job or the promotion you have been waiting for. This is could very well be a premonition of your spell unfolding. Take the time to journal about your dreams or reflect on the emotions that are triggered within the dreamscape, for like omens, the dream language can often be subtle in passing on messages from our Higher Self. We may experience a feeling of positivity or happiness after a dream, and this can be an indication of the spell manifesting, or if the adverse of with unpleasant or uncomfortable dreams we can learn from these dreams about how to increase our magic next time, or what we must cleanse in our life to open ourselves to receiving the magic.

Synchronicities and coincidences will begin to manifest in daily life. Pay close attention to the coincidences that begin to unfold, for often we just brush it off as a coincidence. Yet again this is another indication that you magic is beginning to work. An example of this may be, just after we have cast a spell of candle magic, we receive a call from a past lover or an old friend, that we haven't heard from in a long time. This is a clear sign that your magic has been received by the universe and beginning to unfold. The more we tune into these coincidences and synchronicities the greater our connection to our intuitive psychic abilities become.

Allowing us to truly increase our connectivity with magic. We may even begin to receive these messages through visions or meditative states as we strengthen this bond.

The physical manifestation of our spells may even come as clearly as life encounters. We may begin to meet people unexpectedly who offer us a new project or job, right after we have cast a spell for more money. Sometimes we could even perform a spell for our career and receive a phone call for a new job interview straight after, these are clear indications that our spell is beginning to work. Take advantage of the opportunities that are arising, they may be there just to strengthen your faith and show you spell work is working. Keep moving forward with the magic and watch it grow. When we receive these manifestations of our magic or any signs from above, take the time to give thanks to your magic. This gratitude and acceptance of the magic will also assist in future spells. As you begin to build this confidence and recognize the patterns in the universe responding to your magic begin to refine your own craft and amplify the magic as you continue down the path of becoming a powerful witch.

When you beginning to dive into the craft of spellcasting Wiccan tradition emphasizes making the spell one's own to truly have the most potent effect. For as we have seen, one of the two key factors of spell casting is our intent. So, we often must refine the spell in a unique way to honor our intent. At first as you begin down the path it is recommended to look for spells with clearly laid our instructions and path to follow, so you can begin to understand the process of magic. Yet as you become more adept at the craft, take the time to refine your own spells. Some of the ways we can refine our craft may include:

- Meditating, journaling or a process of reflection that allows introspection after the spell has been cast. Take the time for self-inquiry, this will help deepen your connection with your intuition and build confidence moving forward.

- Notice which parts of the spell casting felt heavy or light, fluid or static, the elements that felt heavy leave them out of your magic casting for now. This is the intuition telling you it is not in alignment with your higher self.

- Meditate, visualize and move the connect to the energy. As we have already explored these techniques practicing our visualization and connection to energy can be a powerful way to increase our spellcraft. Work on your visualization, could you have been more connected to the intent of your spell. The more vividly you can feel the spell has already worked the faster the universe will respond. Review the chapter on *Casting a Circle* and work with these techniques to increase the potency of your spellcasting.

- Find the ingredients, methods, tools and spells that speak to you personally, begin to observe and trust this intuitive flow. Do you feel that you could replace the cinnamon incense with rose in your next love spell? Experiment and trial this, notice which feels more like your essence. You may begin to notice that you prefer candle magic over crystal magic, or possibly you are a kitchen witch working with herbalism or you may even be a Wiccan who prefers to use only intent and energy magic. Honor your path and the magic will flow.

- Change the magic tools or ingredients. If a spell calls for a crystal, yet you prefer to work with herbs, or candle magic, switch the crystal to an herbal counterpart or corresponding candle. For example for abundance spells the spell may call for a green aventurine crystal, yet you prefer to work with basil or patchouli to attract abundance, you may feel more drawn to use a green candle in place of the crystal, or even the combination of all threes, this is perfectly ok to change to and even encouraged within Wicca.

- Work with the Universal timing. Perhaps your spell wasn't as successful as you would have liked and you have changed the intent, or magical tools and still to no avail. Have you looked at the timing of casting? Work with the moon phases to increase the potency of your spell. Note in your grimoire the moon phase at which you cast the spell was it during the New Moon, Waxing Moon, Waning or Full Moon phase, how do you feel this affected your spellcraft? The next time you try this notice what happens on a different moon phase. Keep in mind we have 8 moon phases that the Wiccan tradition will honor. There is exceptional moon charting for spellcraft guides, yet a brief overview may look like this:

- New Moon- Set goals, Sacred Spaces or prepare altar.
- Waxing Moon- Money spells, career spells or moon spells for water.
- First Quarter- Love spells, luck spells and healing spells.
- Waxing Moon- Reflection period, observe your magic and wait.
- Full Moon- Take chances, a time for any form of spells. Perfect for a new spell recipe!
- Waning Moon- Banishing spells, cleansing or detoxing spells and protection spells.
- Last Quarter- Spells for rest, rejuvenation and justice spells.

o Waning Crescent- Look back at the lunar month, time to practice gratitude.

Chapter 5: Good Luck Spells

Simple Chant- *"A clover here, a penny there. Good luck finds me everywhere!"*

Power words for luck- *"Good luck follows me wherever I go."*

Good luck spells have been a tradition throughout all corners of the earth since the beginning of time. Whether this is creating relics, symbols, rituals or superstition to draw more luck into your life these traditions have always held a place within the magic communities. Who does not wish to draw more luck into their life? Of course, we must also have focus and also work towards the results we want yet, this little extra boost from the universe is always appreciated. As we move forward this is a side to acknowledge however, whilst we may cast spells for luck or create amulets, we must also participate actively in drawing our own luck into our lives at times.

Wiccans will even look at the definition of luck in a different way too many people. For within the craft there is the understanding that "luck" is merely a term used by people for the many random gifts from God or the Universe. Yet Wiccan belief claims to have a deeper understanding of what this truly is. Thus, good luck spells are tools to simply attract more gifts from the universe. These spells are designed to help draw in abundance, success or wealth, and as the magic begins to unfold you will notice people saying "you're so lucky" far more frequently, yet you will know the subtly of your magic is at play.

Fu Yishi- Lucky coin Amulet

Heralding from talisman magic one can make a coin amulet to call upon good luck and fortune into your life. This spell is to be performed on the Full Moon to help stay protected from bad luck and simultaneously draw in the good luck.

You will require:

7 Chinese coins

Sandalwood incense

7 Fresh Bay leaves

1 Yellow candle

Red string or ribbon

How to create your magic amulet

1. Place the 7 coins on your altar or magic working table, in the formation of a circle.
2. In the center of your coin circle place the yellow candle and light it.
3. Place the sandalwood incense also in the center to purify the coins and candlelight.
4. Look to the Moon or visualize its fullness if you can't see it. Holding the intent of luck and complete faith in the spell say the following:

    > "*Full Moon, you reveal and advise.*
    > *Tonight, let my petition reach the skies.*
    > *Make your enormous power reach my home*
    > *And enchant these coins.*
    > *Let them protect and fill me with love and joy.*
    > *I am surrounded by your fortune and bliss.*
    > *As I will, so mote it be!*"

5. Crush one of the Bay leaves and rub it into your hands, spreading the aroma over your skin. Take time to smell the leaf and feel the sensations that arise from its fragrance, continue this with the remaining Bay leaves one at a time.

6. Taking the coins, tie them together with the red ribbon or string. As you are tying them together repeat the chant from above thrice.

7. Once your coins are tied together place them back on the altar next to the candle and allow them to remain there until the candle has burnt out. Now you have a good luck amulet to protect and draw good fortune into your life.

Traditional Good Luck Spell

This is a traditionally Wiccan spell, that is easy to practice at any time and perfect for the beginning spellcaster to access some beginners luck through magic! Casting this spell during a full or waxing moon will also enhance the luck of the spell. This spell is for drawing luck in all forms that best serve you, so keep an open mind to how this luck may manifest in your life. With this open heart and open mind, you will open yourself to receiving new opportunities and unexpected elements of luck into your life.

To cast you will require:

Frankincense resin or incense

3 orange or gold spell candles

Pen and paper

To cast the spell:

1. Gather all your items, cleanse you space and cast your circle, being sure to focus on your intention already begin to grow as you cast the circle.

2. Once the circle is cast, light your incense and allow the fragrance to surround your circle.

3. Place the candles in a triangular formation, this shape is a representation of luck, do not light the candles yet.

4. Now your ceremonial space is set recite the following:

"God and Goddess, Spirits and Guides
Thank you for all that I have
I ask you now for (the aspect of life you
need to draw in luck)
Aid me as I work to achieve it
Please bring it to me when the time is right
So mote it be."

5. Take a moment to visualize what your life would be like once you receive this luck that you are asking for. Allow yourself to sit in this sensation of already receiving the good fortune, luck, success, achievement, joy or whatever you are calling in.

6. As you sit with this sensation feel it grow within your chest. Meditate on this feeling and go deep within yourself through this meditation. Continue with this and you will notice a symbol or maybe an image appear within your minds eye. The moment this symbol appears, whatever form it takes, draw this on your paper do not worry about the perfection of the image just allow it to represent your image that you saw.

7. After drawing this, take your piece of paper and lay it within the center of your triangle of candles.

8. Now is the time to light your candles and as you do recite the following with each candle:

"Fire, ignite my dream, for the highest good."

9. Sitting with the candles, watch the flames move and visualize this newfound luck coming your way. Keeping this open heart and mind to how the luck will come, focus more on the intent of the luck itself coming to your rather than exactly how it will come to you. Allow yourself to trust the Universe will bring this luck in the ways that serves your highest self.

10. Stay within this feeling of growing luck and give gratitude to the God and Goddess for what they have

already given you within life for three minutes, noticing how this sensation grows throughout this time.

11. From here take the piece of paper and bury it within the Earth, with this incantation:

"Earth, seal my dream, for the highest good."

12. Now you have finished your ritual, close the circle and allow the candles to burn out casting your new luck into the cosmos to return to you.

Good Luck Spell for Another

Keeping in the tradition of Wicca to bring the ways of truth and love to all beings, this is a potent cauldron spell that will draw luck into the life of another. This spell is a ceremonial spell that does take some practice and knowledge to perform yet is still an excellent addition for a performing adept or even advancing Wiccan. For the beginning Wiccan this is your chance to advance you connection with your cauldron and dive deep into the craft.

You will require:

Cauldron

Mint Leaves

Good Luck powder

Green spell candle

A Key

Sun Oil

Ginger Root

Ginseng Root

High John the conqueror root

Light bulb

Pen and paper

Casting your spell:

1. Begin by dressing your cauldron. This is done by
   adding a few drops of the sun oil to the cauldron. Take
   a moment to rub this in with your hands as you begin
   to channel the intent for your magic. Next rub the
   ginger root along the bottom of your cauldron.
   Followed by adding ginseng root, High John and mint
   leaves to the cauldron.

2. Mix all these magical ingredients together with your
   hands to infuse your energy into the spell work. If you

wish you can add money powder or good luck powder as a final ingredient.

3. Taking the pen and paper, write a petition for the person the spell is intended for, stating what you wish to attract into their lives through this spell. You can even let the other person know you are casting this spell for them and request they write their own petition.

4. Once you have this intent written out, add it to the cauldron. Mix the paper in with the contents of the cauldron like you did before. Add ritual oil as the final step.

5. Next begin to dress and prepare your candle. You may wish to use your sun oil, the luck powder or any additional herbs to amplify this potency of this spell. This is your chance to cultivate some of your own energy into the spell and increase the magic working towards your intent.

6. Now with everything prepared take time to meditate over the cauldron, calling upon any deities, spirits or elements you may work with. Add the key and light bulb into this practice, to increase the clarity of the spell for the other person. Continuing to focus on your intent of manifesting good luck into the cauldron and magical ingredients.

7. Finally place the candle atop of the elements within the cauldron. Still holding your intent in your focus light, the candle and allow it to burn down, as it burns the fire will bring the petition into manifestation and release the magic into the cosmos.

Now you have the tools to cultivate luck within your own life and those around you. Remember the deeper understanding within the Wiccan way towards luck. This will guide you through life to follow and connect with the cosmos and receive the gifts of life along your path. May these spells help you continue on your path of love, magic and light. By honoring these gifts and opening ourselves to this form of "luck" we truly allow the Wiccan way to move through our entire being. Enjoy receiving the gifts of the universe and remember to always keep an open heart, body and mind whilst holding a sense of being in a receiving energy, for this will be the true secret to cultivating more lucky magic in your life.

Chapter 6: Protection Spells

Sometimes we find that we are influenced by negative or evil spirits or toxic relationships and need to rid this toxicity out of our lives. Therefore, we practice the art of banishing magic and protection spells. However, this magic can take time to master. Once mastered these spells of protection and banishment they will become a cornerstone of your witchcraft and an excellent addition to your growing Book of Shadows. With this intention the following spells and enchantments are offered as a guide to help you along the way. Like all forms of magic however the key is to practice and have patience, for many of these spells seemingly simple take time to master and do call upon a calm clear mind to perform otherwise they are easily tainted with the wrong energy. Take your time practicing these ways and you will master the ways of staying calm and collected whilst drawing in more positive energy to your life.

Archangel Michael Protection Enchantment

Connecting with the spirit realms, enchanted beings and Archangels can be a common practice for many Wiccans. Archangel Michael is known as the angel of protection and cutting cords, amongst many other beliefs. He is often depicted with his sword in which many call upon him to cut old ties, release old relationships and even seek protection behind him. This is a spell to call Michael into your life and give this strength and protection whilst also being cleansed of old patterns.

You will simply need a purple feather as a symbol of Archangel Michael, you may wish to find one in nature or merely purchasing one will suffice too.

Casting your spell:

1. With your feather find a space in nature, under direct sunlight is best. Holding the feather to your heart begin to envision that which you wish to cleanse or call in protection from- this may be as simply as a thought, emotion or an idea you do not need to over-specify here, Michael will know what to do.
2. Once you have your intent and still holding the feather to your heart call upon Michael with the following chant:

"Michael, I call to you
With an open heart.
I ask you to protect me.
With your mighty sword,
Shield me from all harm.

3. Then take the feather in your power hand with an open palm, offering the feather to the heavens and recite:

"Bathe me in your warming energy.
Light as a feather, through you,
I am healed, inside and out."

4. Then take a moment to turn inside, scanning your body, spirit and mind. Notice the warmth, tingling in either the hands or feet, possibly flushed cheeks or even a warmth bubbling inside and a smile forming. These are all subtle signs and traits of Michael listening and answering your call. Do not be disheartened if you do not notice this immediately, it can often come in the following 24 hours, allow yourself to remain open and move forth with confidence and strength with this new protecting light watching over you.

Hickory Tree of Protection Spell

A simple spell that has existed for centuries and heralds from Appalachian folklore. Yet this form of folk magic has been honored for its power and ability to break curses and repel the ways of negative magic, through its protective qualities. Perfect for an elemental witch or one who wishes to call upon nature for healing, for all you need is a Hickory tree, a full moon and intent.

Casting your spell:

1. Wait for the eve of a full moon a connect with the Hickory tree.
2. Whilst the moon is at its brightest announce to the tree the name of one whom hexed you, or any intentions that you hold. If you do not know the origin of a curse or problem, merely state what is occurring that you need be freed from.
3. Find a flexible branch or twig that you can easily break off and do so. Then bend and twist said twig tightly and say:

"As I twist and turn this switch, your power is bound, but I be free."

4. Place the bent and twisted branch onto the ground. Give the tree thanks and gratitude for its cleansing ways and

return directly home. Your hex will be cleansed by the setting of the moon.

Rosemary Home Blessing

Blessing and protecting our homes can be a powerful tool and a common practice of Wiccans from all traditions. Working with some simple herbal magic we can cultivate an atmosphere of pure love, healing and protection. Rosemary is one such herb that has been honored for holding all of these properties by cultures throughout all time periods. With this magical herb we can bring these qualities into our homes and daily life.

You will require:

Dried bundle of rosemary

A bowl of purified water

Purple piece of string

Casting you spell:

1. Begin by smudging your home or space that you wish to cast this protection spell in. Be sure to also smudge your rosemary bundle. You can even smudge the space

with another rosemary bundle to amplify the power of this magic.

2. Then taking your protection bundle and bowl of water repeat the following blessing:

"Hear me rosemary
Allow it to be
Through shine love, health or wealth
May keep me always free
So mote it be."

3. Then dip the rosemary into the bowl of water and use it to lightly sprinkle water throughout your house or space to be protected. Move in a clockwise direction as you make your way around the space.

4. The entire time holding you intent in focus and feeling the cleansing you are bringing to your home.

5. Once you have covered the whole space thank the spirit of the herb and take the purple string to hang the bundle by a doorframe or window to keep the protection within the room.

6. Finally tip the remaining water from the bowl into your front garden to add the protection from the front of the house and into the space.

7.

Bad Luck Be Gone

There is moments in our life where we have a period of bad luck or a series of unfortunate events. We may need to cleanse this streak or even call more luck into our lives to balance some of this misfortune. Otherwise if we continue down this unfortunate path, we may open ourselves to bad energies, or receiving a curse from another, which is often the reason for the mysterious unlucky streak. Fortunately, the Wiccan way has encountered this before, and we can cleanse and clear this bad luck. This is a spell to break this rather vicious cycle of events, without trying to get even with someone else, allowing forgiveness to take precedent.

You will require:

> A piece of parchment
>
> Black inked pen
>
> Cauldron
>
> Green pillar candle

Casting your spell:

1. Begin with cleansing your house and magical tools, or any spaces that you feel may be accumulating this unfortunate luck- including yourself.

2. Cast a circle to keep the intent clear in a sacred space.

3. Now on the parchment record a summarized version of your bad luck streak or any attributes that have called for the need of this spell.

4. Next, light your candle. Offering the parchment to the candle until it catches fire. Then drop the parchment in your cauldron (being careful not to burn yourself).

5. Visualizing the bad luck being transformed by the flame repeat the following nine times:

"Misfortunes of the recent past
Are burning now, they will not last."

6. Immediately extinguish your candle, putting an end to this bad luck. Close your circle and step into a period of new-found luck and joy.

The Banishment of Waxing Moon Spell

When we begin to explore the realms of Wicca we begin to understand the subtler workings that the spiritual realms also play into our daily life. Working with the lunar calendar we connect with the Goddess energy to help cleanse and clear. This banishing spell whilst sounding simple my take some time to master, be patient and only work with this spell on the waxing moon or it may affect the intent of the spell.

You will require:

Apple cider vinegar

Dried Rosemary, Thyme & Mint

3 cloves fresh garlic

A mason jar

Casting you spell:

1. On the evening of a waxing moon gather all your ingredients for this magical banishing jar.
2. Find a quiet space and cast your circle. Take the time to center, ground and enter a clear meditative state setting your intention with complete clarity.
3. Begin by placing the herbs in the mason jar first, then followed by the garlic bulbs and finally the apple cider vinegar on top to cover the herbs and garlic. Screw the lid on to make the jar airtight.
4. Gentle shake the jar to activate the alchemical magic within.
5. Closing your eyes focus on the entity or situation you need to banish from your life, staying within this calm focused state you cultivated earlier.
6. Feel your energy beginning to fill the rest of the jar. Once you can envision this jar being filled with your

energy leave it in a dark, cool space for the following lunar month.

7. Finally, when the time arises. Open the jar- be warned it will not smell nice. Then sprinkle in your garden, on our doorstep and windowsill to cleanse and banish these negative entities

Now you have the tools, the ways and the insight to cultivate this protective energy into your blossoming craft. May you move forth with a clear, focused and pure intent to continue cultivating your magic. If the time arises that you feel you need to recast any of these spells, first wait one lunar month (28 days) before recasting as banishing and protection can take time to grow.

Chapter 7: Spells for health

"Wrap thee in cotton, bind thee with love.

Protection from pain surrounds like a glove.

May the brightest of blessings surround thee on this night

For thou art cared for, healing thoughts are sent to you in flight."

-Healing chant for yourself and another

The realms of healing magic are vast and can take many forms. When diving into these forms' spells may range from candle magic, incantations, healing herbs, herbal teas, baths, rituals and ceremonies. Yet within all these vast forms of magic one must remember this is not a replacement for pharmaceutical care or to replace the advice of a doctor for serious illness, as most forms of spellcraft works on the prevention of illness or aiding already used healing methods. Here we will explore various spells to aid in general wellbeing, gaining more focus and clarity, methods of increasing vitality in life and investigate spells related to healing. For further information on healing herbs within Wiccan also explore my book, *Wiccan Herbalism: Beginner Grimoire* for more in-depth healing guides to the healing realms of herbs.

Through an understanding of body, mind and spirit we gain begin to see a connection of how our emotions, thoughts and actions all affect our general health and wellbeing. Hence, we use these forms of magical healing arts to align our energetic and physical body through natural practices, energies and holistic healing to live a with a greater sense of wholeness and wellness within all aspects of life. Even in turn teaching others to live this way and share the magic with those we come into contact with.

Healing spells and magic are not only aspects of the craft we use on ourselves but also spread to others. We may use these forms of magic for an energetic boost, to aid our healing process or whenever we are faced with difficulties in life. This could be as simple as connecting to crystal magic, working with Amethyst or Rose Quartz. We may take time in nature to connect with the elements to realign ourselves with the natural order of the cosmos. Simply taking a walk barefoot in nature can help ground ourselves into the earth and flood the system with the medicine that lay within Gaia, or we may even call upon rituals, ceremonies and the wisdom of old to return to our truest self. The world of healing magic and possibilities is endless, so take your time to explore, connect and share the healing love to allow for healing of not only yourself but all beings as was intended by Gardner when he bought the Wiccan way into the mainstream light.

Please note: This book and the knowledge contained within these pages are true and practical to the authors and publisher's knowledge, however for diagnosis or treatment for ailments, injuries, illness or any medical related problem, one must still consult their own physician and seek professional medical opinion. This is a key within all spells we must also take other measure to assist the magic realms where we can. Some Wiccans will decide that this is the only form of healing they need, yet you will often find that they have extensive knowledge of herbalism, nutrition and awareness of the elements around them. Be sure to seek consultation from a professional, as the publisher and author are not responsible for any specific health, allergy or ailment needs that may require medical supervision and are not liable for negative consequences or damages from any spells, treatments, action, application or preparation from the information provided within this book. Please keep in mind these spells, information and knowledge within this book are correct according to our tradition and practice, yet it is at the discretion of the reader to use the information provided by their own right and responsibility.

Spell for focus and improved memory

This is a simple spell perfect for an initiate on the path. By casting this spell you will be able to increase focus and memory, assisting in daily life as well as any future craft you wish to create. All you need for this spell is a yellow pillar candle and regular practice. You will require 9 day's time to perform this spell.

Casting the spell:

1. Begin your magic on a Thursday, repeating this spell over nine consecutive days to allow the magic to flow.
2. Light your yellow candle and concentrate on this yellow color, associated with memory.
3. Once in a meditative state on this candle recite the following five times;

"Oh cheerful yellow, penetrate my mind,
Improve my memory give me powers of great
observation.
May I remember all I seek to recall,
May my concentration be perfect in all things
big and small."

4. Repeat this process over the eight following days (nine in total) using the same yellow candle each time.

5. Any time you need to recall this focus and clear your mind take three deep breaths envisioning the yellow candle, allow this magic to flow through you in moments of recollection.

Traditional Spell for Good Health

Working with the old wives tale *"An apple a day will keep the doctor away,"* this spell not only works with the health benefits of apples but also honoring that they are an ancient symbol for health. Thus, we instantly give homage to the ways of old through keeping this magic alive. When choosing your apple for this spell the riper, firmer and juicer the apple the more potency the spell will bring to manifest your good health. This is a simple spell yet one that has been passed down through the ages thanks to the belief of its potency even for a beginner Wiccan.

You will require:

Juice red apple

Athame or paring knife

Casting your spell:

1. Taking your apple very carefully carve your name and date of birth into the skin of the apple. On the opposing side carve a simple star for the 5 elements.

2. Continue by cutting your apple in half and eat both halves. As you eat each half of your apple contemplate the natural formation of the star that occurs when you cut an apple in half. Recite the following whilst consuming the apple (either between bites or mentally will also work):

"May my heart ache no more
My body be not sore
May my health be with me to my very core"

3. When you have finished eating your apple and recited the above incantation thrice. Bury the apple core under the biggest tree within your garden or the nearest to your garden.

Healing light for another

A beautiful spell to help a speedy recovery for another whether this be physical or mental illness this is a spell used throughout the craft to bring healing to another in need. Keeping in mind this form of magic will aid the persons recovery process, yet if the person with illness themselves does not wish to recover the spell may not produce results. Upon casting this spell you can enhance the power by also working with the full moon imagining the illness reducing or on the new moon envisioning the person returning to full health.

You will require:

A human-shaped candle, based on the gender of the intended person

Myrrh or Mint oil

A photograph of the person

Casting your spell:

1. Begin by cleansing your sacred space, being sure to purify your magical objects including the photograph of the ill person. Casting a circle can amplify the magic yet is not necessary for this spell.
2. Begin by writing the name of the ill person onto the candle. Followed by anointing the candle with the Myrrh or mint oil. During the dressing of your candle begin to visualize white healing light beginning to flow from your fingers into the candle charging the candle with this healing energy.
3. Before lighting your candle recite the following:

"In the divine names of the Goddess,
Who breathes life into us all
I consecrate and charge this candle
As a magical tool for healing."

4. Now place the candle on top of the photograph of the person with the illness. Light the candle whilst focusing on this healing energy sparking inside of them.

5. Take time to reflect on this person as this candle burns down. Concentrating on this person imagine the healing energy flowing to their being and chant the following incantation:

"Magic mend and candle burn,
Sickness end, good health return."

6. Continue chanting this incantation and visualizing this healing energy flooding to the person until the candle burns down. Close your circle and allow the magic of your spell work to fill this person with rejuvenated energy.

Dream quartz healing spell

A powerful spell for aiding in deep sleep when you are tired, stressed or need the extra rest for healing. Many cultures and traditions believe sleep is one of the greatest healing tools we can utilize. With this in mind this spell allows us to calm the mind and rest the body with a deep night's sleep. This spell is also renowned for working on restoring your inner strength as it is also for promoting healing and rejuvenation to all aspects of the body, making it the ideal spell for recouping from any illness. Many Wiccans will even write out or print this spell to have by their bedside table to access on those evening of restless sleep.

You will require:

Lavender sprigs- fresh or dry

Smoky Quartz

A blank piece of parchment- Traditionally it is said parchment is needed for this spell rather than blank paper, yet you can interchange if need be.

To cast your spell:

1. This first step is optional to increase the potency of the spell. By refreshing your room and bed with fresh bedsheets, quietness and dimmed lights or candlelight one can focus deeper on the spell and enhance the quality of sleep.

2. Take a moment to sit on your bed holding the smoky quartz, be sure to be seated comfortably yet avoid the sitting on the pillow that you will rest your head on shortly.

3. Over a few minutes, focus simply on the grounding energy of your quartz. Visualize the stone sending any troubling thoughts into the earth.

4. Once you feel centered and grounded from your crystal, take the crystal in the right hand only moving the wrist clockwise thrice whilst reciting the following with each rotation of your wrist:

"The moon is up, I hold its piece,
the silver dust will guide my peace."

5. After you have recited the following three times and moved your wrist wrap the crystal in with the rosemary sprigs and parchment. Place this next to your bed or under your pillow (depending how big the quartz is).

Note: You can practice this spell as frequently as needed. Keep in mind that all spell work takes time. Do not be disheartened or discouraged if you do not see results straight away. Thank yourself for the attempt and connecting with your spell work, revise the ways you could improve with your knowledge that you are now developing and then try again the following evening. This "Dream Quartz Healing Spell" has been used throughout many cultures including South American cultures as the stone itself is known for its healing grounding properties, so keep in mind the magic may be working on a very subtle level that we often miss at first.

Let this healing magic work through you and may these spells bring wealth, health and wellbeing in all forms. Through these spells the power of your wellbeing is within your hands. Take the time to notice the changes that you can make in your lifestyle to also help the spells work their magic, your intuition will whisper this truth to you. Yet, do seek further medical assistance in times of need, for this information is but a guide to wellbeing and wellness to the best of this authors path and knowledge. Through this responsibility and balance you can truly cultivate the lifestyle you choose. Including sharing this knowledge with others in your life, encouraging them to cultivate magic in alignment with their health. You may even wish to explore more Wiccan magic that promotes further healing through the magic of herbs, remedies and tradition of old for natural healing, if so continue look into my other book *Wiccan Herbalism A Beginners Grimoire*. This holds seeks, knowledge and wisdom from the ways of old and insights as to how the magic of herbs can really shape our health and the society around us. Including its influence on modern medicine.

Chapter 8: Love Spells

Let us uncover the mysteries and realms of love spells. For some this is the appeal to spellcraft itself, whether you are looking for a new romance or rekindle an ex-relationship there are many ways we can work with magic to access more love in our life. Love spells or love magic is one of the greatest magical tools to also cultivate self-empowerment. Through spell casting and forms of meditation you can take the time to truly reflect on which is the best path for you moving forward. Keep in mind that one should not wish to change another's path to benefit our own, we should always use this magic to open ourselves more. Thus, the spells we will explore here are designed to affect and work on oneself rather than alter the ways of another. For as we open our own heart and vibration to this vibration of love, we allow more love to flow our way, from this space we may find that rekindling of a fleeting love, or a new romance blossoms within our life.

As love spells require very specific and clear intent traditionally these spells were cast by healers and shamans. Yet over the centuries the methods for connecting to this magic has become more open within the Wiccan way. As we begin to connect with love magic, it is always beneficial to take time in introspection first through meditation to connect and communicate with your higher self to become in alignment with your intuition. Coming into this alignment will always guide you to the greatest joy, sometimes from an unexpected outcome. A love spell is believed within the Wiccan way to always align your body, heart and mind by bringing your feet back onto the ground, as for from here you will attract exactly that which you deserve and need, no more or less.

Some of the most effective love spells include chanting, prayers or mantras and even affirmations that reinforce this opening to love. This may be as simple as writing an affirmation of *'I attract the love I deserve into my life'* or *'Love and abundance flows to me in all moments, with an open heart, open mind and open soul. I am Love.'* These affirmations an inner form of magic changing our subconscious to open ourselves to this vibrational energy. The yogis use the mantra *Ahem Prema,* meaning 'I am love', to open themselves to this flow of love. For our first step is to believe we deserve the magic that we cultivate otherwise the spell has no power, once we believe then the magic can unfold. Additionally, we can use ritual magic to draw this love into our lives whether that be improving our romantic relationship, recovering a lost love, attracting a new love or opening ourselves to more love in life. Let us explore a few spells to help get us started and then you can continue to explore, experiment and refine your own craft to make your practice.

Red Candle Love Spell

One of the oldest spells in the book of love. This magic spell has been passed down the lines in many traditions since the ways of old, taking many forms and expressions over time. This is a spell that works with a unique form of magic often called *Red Magic*, also referred to as the magic of love and spirituality, a type of magic that resides between the realms of white and black magic, calling on the knowledge from both. Yet this spell is known to leave no negative energy after casting, whilst still having powerful potent results when cast with the correct intent. This is a spell that you can cast to call in a new love to your life or even to strengthen a new growing relationship, this spell responds to the caster's intention.

All you will require is 1 red candle and a clean focused intention.

To cast your spell:

1. Wait until dusk, find a dim and quiet place at home to light your candle.

2. Allow yourself to be seated in a meditative state watching the flickering flame. Allow the feeling of love to arise within you, around you and eventually filling the entire space that surrounds you.

3. Once you can feel this love surrounding you, repeat the following incantation twelve times over:

"I ask the Forces of the Universe,
I ask the spirits
I ask the Angels watching over me
To help this love grow stronger."

4. Upon finishing this incantation return to watching the flame. Reconnecting with this feeling of growing love around you and noticing how it has completely filled not only the space around you but also continued to expand.

5. As you watch the candle envision the flame burning away any negative thoughts you that come to mind or emotions and notice how the flame of the red candle transforms them into loving energy.

6. Take the time to thank the elements and continue to cultivate this sensation of love until the candle naturally burns out.

7. Whenever you feel the sensation of love depleting within you simply visualize the flickering flame and this

transforming spell to cultivate the sensation of love inside your heart again.

Note: This is an ancient spell with the words translated from the scripts of old, hence the incantation does not rhyme as many newer spells will. Be sure to say each word correctly in the right order, or your spell is unlikely to work. If you mispronounce a word or confuse the order, blow out your candle, close the circle and try again at a later time.

Amber Love Magnet

Heralding from the Roman Gypsy tradition, and since adopted onto the Wiccan beliefs this talisman magic works to attract a new lover into your life. Whilst this spell is intended to work for attracting love into your own life, one could also cast this spell for another and gift them the *"Amber Love Magnet."* This is a perfect beginners magic spell with powerful effects. For this spell all you need is 1 amber stone and a Red pouch or sachet, and of course the right intent. *It is recommended to cast this spell on a Sunday evening to open yourself to the love throughout the week.*

To cast the spell:

1. Cleanse your amber stone in water to purify its energy and charge it with the intent to attract love.

2. Scribe on a piece of paper the qualities you wish to attract with your new love, and attributes you want in a soulmate.

3. Place the amber stone under your pillow to sleep with for 3 nights. Leaving this on your altar for some time or meditating with it for a few days first can increase the potency.

4. After the 3rd morning bring the stone close to your heart, with your left hand. At this time keeping a clear intention for the magic and pure emotions of love.

5. Visualize a bubble of love growing inside of you, imagining that you have already attracted this love unto you and feeling the amount of love you will share with your new partner. You do not need to focus on a specific person, yet just the sensation of the love, if you can. Spending the feels of joy, happiness and love to this amber stone.

6. Put the Amber stone into your silk pouch, to carry with you for the following week. Maybe keeping it in you jacket pocket, or on a necklace to be near your heart.

7. Each morning for the following week, continue this visualization exercise and sleep with the pouch under your pillow, watching this love grow each day. Continue to carry this Amber magnet with you until your loved one manifests.

Fire Flowers Love Spell

Working with candle magic and incantation, this is the perfect high magic spell to attract new pathways and connections of love into your life. Used by Wiccans to open themselves to new romance and being able to receive more love, one can find the *"Fire flowers"* throughout most Wiccan traditions. Traditional magic such as this spell are exceptional for all levels of magic and introduce a Wiccan to the structure of spellcraft, preparing you to cultivate your own spells.

You will require:

1 Pink Candle

3 White Flowers- daisies, lilies, carnation or another white flower that you choose.

Incense of your tradition- cinnamon, jasmine, roses or ylang-ylang are best for love magic.

Rose or Jasmine Essential Oil

Cauldron

Paper and pencil

Casting the Spell: First create your sacred space with cleansing and casting a circle.

1. Once the circle is cast begin by lighting you incense allowing the fragrance to fill the space.

2. Prepare your candle for the ritual, as this will be your doorway into new love. Take the time to dress the candle with your essential oil. As you dress the candle with oil use the following incantation:

"I clean and consecrate this candle
So that it may serve as a sign
Of the covenant between me
And the Element of Fire.

3. Light the candle and place in a candle holder or dish within your circle.

4. Take the first flower, gentle begin to remove one petal at a time until none remain. As you do this continue to breathe deeply and slowly feeling the vibration of love whilst saying:

5.

"I am (inhale)
Full of power (exhale)
A powerful love (inhale)
That burns like fire (exhale)"

6. Repeat this with the remaining flowers, until all three flowers are petal-less. Place all the petals into your

cauldron. Throughout this time clear your mind of any thoughts or worries, allowing yourself to become rare and bare like the buds of the flower.

7. On the paper, write your full name and intent.

8. Light the piece of paper, using the candles flame. Place the burning paper into the cauldron on top of the flower petals.

9. Watching the paper and petals burn say thank you to the magic of transformation opening you to love. Allow the candle to fully burn holding this stable presence and intent.

10. Bury the remains of the ashes and any remaining petals from your cauldron, either burying them in the garden of a potted flower.

11. Close your circle and allow the magic of love flow into your being.

Full Moon Love Spell

This is a full moon love spell to be cast under the moonlight of the full moon. Yet another powerful Wiccan spell from the ways of old to attract new love into your life. A clear intent is required for this spell, so prior to performing make sure you are clear on what type of relationship you wish to call into your life. When focusing on this intent do not become stuck on the finer details, yet rather the overall feeling. For example, if you wish to attract someone compassionate and loving, focus on the feelings of love and compassion rather than specific ways the person will embody these traits.

You will require:

    1 Red spell candle

    1 Pink spell candle

    Dried basil

    Ground cinnamon

    Two apple seeds

    1 Moonstone crystal

    1 Rose quartz crystal

    Piece of red cloth

    Pink cord or string

Casting your spell:

1. After you have set your intent wait for the next full moon. Gather all your magical ingredients and create sacred space underneath the full moonlight, and cast your circle being sure to have everything with you first.

2. Light both your candles whilst laying the red cloth in front of you.

3. First take the moonstone and pass it through the flame of the white candle then the pink candle and place the crystal on the red cloth. Repeat this with the rose quartz crystal.

4. Take in your hands the two apple seeds, and recite:

   "By the light of the moon, I now plant the seeds of love."

5. As you say this place the seeds onto the cloth, visualizing a beautiful pink energy pulsing and radiating from the crystals washing over the seeds with pure vibrations of love.

6. Take a moment to sprinkle the basil and cinnamon onto the seeds and crystals, the whole time feeling the growing love.

7. Once all these materials are in place on the red cloth, take the corners of the cloth and fold them in on each other, holding the crystals, herbs and seeds within. After folding the red cloth in a bundle, take the pink cord or string and tie it thrice around the bundled cloth, tying three knots around it. With the third knot stating, *"So mote it be."*

8. Now you can close your circle, thanking the Goddess and the moon. Keep your new charm with you to attract newfound love into your life.

Endless Desire

A bottle spell to strengthen a current relationship. This is a positivity charging spell working on removing any negative energy or blockages in a relationship. This is a potent love spell to help you fix or redeem a broken relationship or ideally increase a partner's commitment within the relationship. Without the need for incense, or candle magic this spell works with a witch bottle recipe, that makes a powerful charm. Making it an easy spell to cast at any time from home. Believed to keep a husband or wife loyal, or even work on friendships and other relationships too.

You will require:

> 1 glass bottle with a lid
>
> 2 Red roses
>
> Paper and pen

Casting the spell:

> 1. Begin by consecrating the bottle and the roses. Then place the two fresh Red Roses inside the bottle.

2. Write the full names of both people in the relationship on the paper and place inside of the bottle.

3. Recite the following incantation as you do:

"Crystals and flowers,
Pact and conspire.
Burn in his/her Heart
With Endless desire."

4. Seal the lid or cork onto the glass bottle. Finally bury the bottle into your garden, or somewhere that no one can find it, like a nearby wood.

5. Leave the magic spell bottle for as long as you want this love to last.

Relationship Healing Spell

This spell is for the keeling aspects of a marriage or relationship through cleansing and clearing. You will need to write two letters in preparation for this spell. One letter is to clear your current emotional state; what is wrong with the relationship? Be as open and honest as you can be, no one but you will see this, and the more honest the more potency the spell will have. So be emotional, angry, sad or whatever needs to come up allow it to flow into this letter. Once you have wrote this note, you will write a second letter. Yet this time from the perspective of how you want the relationship to be. How should your lover act towards you? Do you want them to listen more, talk more, give more attention, open more, anything at all? Again, be open and authentic with your desires here. So, you may come to the final answer of what would make you happy in the relationship?

Once you have wrote these two letters, take some time to re-center and ground your energy. Meditate or smudge yourself so you can be in a clear state for the spell work.

You will require:

    1 White Candle

    1 Pink candle

    Your cauldron (or fireproof vessel)

    Matches

    Pen and paper

    2 Pieces of string

To cast your spell:

1. Once you are calm and grounded after the letter writing, take as much time as you need for this spell will require

clear intent. Cast your circle, being sure to collect all your materials for the spell work before you do, including the letters.

2. Start the spell by lighting the white candle, to represent peace and spirit, then light the pink candle, for affection and love.

3. Taking the first letter (the letting go one) place it in the cauldron. Light it on fire with the matches and watch it burn, visualizing the negative energy being transformed by the fire and cleared as the paper burns. As you watch it burn recite the following:

"Sacred flames, carry these energies away,
Let our relationship begin a new today."

4. Now take the second letter, read through it imagining everything in the letter already happening in this moment. Allowing yourself to visualize you and your spouse happily committed to each other.

5. From here take the two pieces of string and tie them together to form one long piece of string. Being sure to make the knot nice and strong as this represents the connection and bonding of your love. Fold the paper on itself a few times and wrap the string around this second letter. As you wrap this string around the letter, recite:

"God and Goddess above,
Help me reunite with my love.
Bring us loving harmony and peace,
May the strength of our bond increase.
So, mote it be."

6. After you have tied this note with the string and completed your incantation. Close your circle. Take your letter and the string to a tree to be buried (if possible, a birch or apple tree, are known to express love, if not any other tree will.

Now you have the spells, tools and motivation to find new love within your life. Keep in mind that this form of spell casting can be extremely powerful and will reflect our deepest intent. Be sure to keep your intention clear and focused throughout all these spells and keep an open heart to the ways that universe may provide. Remembering that when we work with love magic often, we receive that which will best serve our intent and path, so we occasionally miss the subtly of magic returning to us and this is why an open heart is the key. If we can manage this, we will notice that love flows to us in abundance in many forms and in no time be untied with the truest and purest love that our heart and soul could desire. As this arises may you find all you seek and realize that you are worthy of this deeply profound love.

~Ahem Prema~

Chapter 9: Career & Money Magic Spells

Through the Wiccan tradition we can bring magic into all aspects of our life as we are beginning to see, including into our business. With the practice of various career magic spells, we can call more abundance into our lives and open ourselves to the flow of prosperity. One may work with the lunar cycle to call open this wealth, or candle magic to find a nice business partner or even make talismans to have around the office that magnetize more customers. Whatever you preferred form of spellcraft mainstream business can flourish with some touches of ancient magic wisdom also infused. As you develop this practice the ways of old will even serve as a guiding light into how one should continue to grow, expand and evolve their career in magic ways!

Waxing Moon magic spell

As its name, this is a spell to call in money into your life that needs be cast on the waxing moon, the first quarter of the lunar calendar whilst the moon is gaining light, this is the best time for money magic. Even if you are new at working with moon magic, you can ask a friend for guidance or seek consultation from an adept Wiccan, as most moon magic is simple enough if cast at the right time. When you are at the time of the waxing moon this spell is perfect to cast.

You will require:

> 1 Brown candle- the color of wealth and increase income.
>
> A gold coin
>
> Zest of one orange
>
> Dried basil
>
> 1 Cinnamon stick

Casting you spell:

1. In preparation for your spellcraft creating a small aromatic mix of your herbs. Add the basil, orange zest and cinnamon into a mortar and pestle to crush and blend them together.

2. On the eve of a waxing moon, find a quiet space making sure you have no artificial light but can connect with the natural moonlight. Gather your magical tools and cast your circle.

3. Lighting your candle, focus on the flickering flame. Take 30 deep slow breaths, with each breath imagining the vibration of wealth and prosperity entering your life.

4. Place the gold coin and spices between your palms. Rubbing your hands together take 3 deep breaths of the fragrance from the coin and the aromatic mixture.

5. Recite the following threefold as you focus your intent on the growing wealth and fragrance:

"Money flow, money grow, money glow."

6. Blow out the candle, close your circle. Keep your coin in your wallet or purse and focus on this growing wealth that comes into your life over the coming weeks.

Full Moon Money Magic

If you are a Wiccan who works with moon magic, then this full moon magic can really increase wealth and prosperity in your life. You may wish to work with the above spell on a waxing moon to watch this money grow and then even increase the potency by casting this spell upon the full moon to seal the wealth in your life.

Again, the timing is key to this magic, have the patience for the full moon to enable the true magic to flow.

You will require:

> 3 Gold coins
>
> A red pouch or wallet – here red is for the symbol of good luck, however you can also use a dark brown wallet to represent money.
>
> A small mirror, small enough to fit in the wallet.

Casting your spell:

1. Once the moon is full. Find a quiet dark space, one without artificial light but that the moonlight may fill the space. No other candles, lights or secondly light should be present otherwise your spell may not work.
2. Open the wallet and place the gold coins inside, one at a time. Picturing the wealth coming in as you do so. Last place the mirror inside the wallet. Holding a pure intent and focus the whole time.
3. With the wallet full and now sealed shut. Close your eyes and focus on the flow of energy represented by money. Then say the following incantation thrice:

"Note to note, coin to coin.
The flow of wealth I will soon join."

4. Sit for a moment and feeling the wealth that is coming your way. Thank the Goddess energy of the moon and close your circle. See the wealth flow into your life over the following lunar month.

Job Promotion Spell

This is a spell for helping forward movement in your career, calling in that promotion that you have been working for or a pay rise you deserve, or possibly even receiving a job offer from another employer. This is a spell to give back for the efforts that you are putting in, so be sure to have an honest intention to help the potency of the magic.

You will require:

    1 Beeswax candle

    A large hand full of rolled oats

    9 Bay leaves

    1 Clay pot

Casting your spell:

1. Sit in the center of your circle, cultivating this clear and pure space. Sitting here comfortably close your eyes and begin to focus on all your recent achievements in your role. Noticing the sensation of success beginning to swell inside of you. Take your time to notice this sensation grow in your stomach and mind, sitting in this blissful state.

2. Opening your eyes, add the oats into the clay pot. Light the candle and place it next to the pot.

3. Create a circle around the candle and clay pot with the Bay leaves, dry or fresh either work, as long as the leaves are whole.

4. Recite the following thrice:

"Money, prosperity, wealth, recognition
May my career reach the state of ignition."

5. Again, closing your eyes and visualize receiving this promotion and accepting the position. Focusing your attention on the sensations that arise from receiving this new position, how does the promotion feel, what we you do with the new money, allow this to flood your being.

6. Close your circle and allow the candle to naturally burn itself out, even if you need to move it be careful not to put out the flame.

Luck in Business Magic Spell

This is the perfect spell for that time when you are approaching an upcoming deadline, or about to close a deal with a new business partner. Also, a great spell to remind us how Wicca can be practiced by anyone in any realm. A spell to make sure no matter how good your business ethic is that the universe is on your side.

You will require:

A handful of bay leaves, fresh or dry is ok, just as long as they are whole.

1 Green ribbon

3 Gold coins

Blank piece of parchment

Casting your spell:

1. Crumble the piece of parchment (if not accessible substitute for baking paper), flattening with your hands. Place the gold coins and bay leaves in the middle of the parchment.

2. Fold the sides over and tie your green ribbon around to form a parcel. This will now serve as a good luck charm within your business endeavors.

3. From here close your eyes. Placing the index finger of your power hand onto the parcel. Keeping your finger here and eyes closed spend 5-10 minutes focusing and visualizing your business goals growing with this parcel, the longer you spend the better, as long as the intent stays pure and clear.

4. Finally hide the charm within your office, somewhere only you know where it is and it will be left untouched for your business ventures.

The Magic of Success Spell

A powerful Wiccan spell to bring more success into your life. Perfect in the time of starting a new business venture, to increase your salary, find a new job or even increase your current business venture. This is a powerful white magic spell working in the traditions of high magic.

You will require:

A photo of yourself

4 Green spell candles

1 White spell candle

3 Drops of essential oil that represents your astrological
sign

Amber incense

10 Bay leaves

2 Green fluorite crystals

An offering bowl

Money- preferably a note, any denomination will suffice.

Casting the spell:

1. As this is also a white magic ritual, the caster is called to dress in white. Also, to purify yourself with the essential oil of your astrological sign, cleansing the hands and feet with a few drops.
2. Before casting your circle, place the 4 green candles at the cardinal points, as for the white candle place this in front of where you will be seated.
3. Place the amber incense to the left side of the white candle.
4. Into the offering bowl place the fluorite crystals, bay leaves and banknote together, placing each item one at a time into the bowl.
5. Set the photo in front of the candle.

6. Now that you have everything prepared and set for your ritual, cast your circle around yourself and magical tools. Staying grounded in your circle light each of the green candles first and finally the white candle in front of you. Then lighting the incense with the white candle.

7. Take the white candle and drop a few drops of wax onto your photo. Holding the offering bowl with both hands, the left on top of the right, consecrate your picture.

8. Recite the following incantation to cultivate your personal success thrice:

"Success is coming soon to me,
Prosperity is flowing unto me,
So mote it be."

9. Now sitting in silence begin to visualize the sensation that comes with complete financial freedom. Feeling money flowing to you with ease and abundance. Notice how you are completely and totally in the flow of receiving. Allow these feelings and thoughts to overwhelm you for as long as you can, the longer you can hold these positive thoughts and vibrations the more potent the spell will become. Yet be sure to only hold happy, pure and positive intent during this time.

10. When you feel yourself full of this successful vibration, blow out each of the green candles and the white candle

last. Close your circle, thanking the elements and directions and you do so and allow the incense to keep burning to release this success into the cosmos.

11. After this spell whenever thoughts come to mind about success or money, remember the positive full vibrations. Recall these vibrations of abundance and even recite this incantation in these moments to help you recall the vibration of success. The more you refocus on this the more quickly it will flow into your life.

Attract More Customers

A spell which helps to attract more clientele into your business and bring forth the abundance of financial means this way. This spell is also useful for cleansing the energy of your business, to also allow for the growth in customers. Perfect for the Wiccan who is in competitive business life or growing a business.

You will require:

A business card or a small object that represents your business

1 Beeswax candle (bees are symbolic of prosperity and wealth)

Red ribbon

3 Gold coins

A mason jar

To cast your spell:

1. At your workspace when you are alone, cast a small circle in your office. Light the candle, dim the lights and allow yourself to sit in a state of meditation for 10 minutes.

2. After you are centered, and the mind is clear. With your eyes open continue to watch the flame as it dances for 10 minutes more, the entire time focusing on the mental reasons as to why you have started the business or the intent of your work. Notice any negative thought patterns that arise and offer them to the flame for transformation throughout this time.

3. Place all the objects into the mason jar one at a time while chanting the following incantation:

> *"I serve my purpose day and night,*
> *My soul is bright as candlelight,*
> *My work is honest and sincere,*
> *I want to see more people here."*

4. Once all items are placed within the jar, seal the lid on allowing a thin layer of the candle wax to seal it shut.

5. Place the jar somewhere at your workplace in a hidden space to keep the magic in your business.

Spellcraft to become debt-free

This spell should be cast during the waning or new moon, as it can also be classed as a banishing spell. A spell to banish debt and give abundance when it comes to one's bills.

You will require:

    Pen and paper

    White pillar candle- for purity and cleansing

    Either patchouli, frankincense or sandalwood incense

    A needle

Casting your spell:

1. The first stage of preparation will be to write a list of all your debt, writing down on the paper not only what you owe but also whom you owe it too.

2. After making this list inscribe the same list onto your candle using the needle. Then finish by anointing your candle with 3 drops of the essential oil of your choice.

3. Once these items are prepared gather your tools for the magic casting and create your circle.

4. Light the candle and sit with a still mind, focusing your intent on the candle watching your debt burn away as the flame moves.

5. Using your technique of visualization imagine paying the final bill of your debt. Notice the sensation that arises, notice how it feels to pay this final bill. Focus all your intent on this feeling and vibration that is present. Allowing yourself to sit in this freedom for the following 5 minutes, noticing it grow.

6. Close your circle yet allow the candle to burn for the same duration you sat in meditation, allowing this energy to be released into the universe.

7. Repeat this method and ritual every night until the candle completely burns down and soon you will see yourself released from debt and moving forward with financial freedom.

Note: Stay open the messages from life around that may represent this magic. Keeping an open mind is what allows this magic to take place. It may not be that the debt is just cleansed from your bank account but rather you are given advice on how to save money from a magazine or you may receive a bonus from your job that enables you to pay off this debt. By remaining open you will allow this magic to enchant your life.

May these spells bring your work life the balance and desired abundance you wish to cultivate. With correct intent, right practice and time you will begin to notice clients flooding in, debts clearing away and money rolling in. Be warned that you may even find a strong sense of being overwhelmed at times when these spells truly begin to flow, keep a balanced life and mind through the practices of meditation, visualization and you will begin to navigate the magic that lays within your spells. If this happens, accept closing one spell for some time, and then recasting as you see fit, there is nothing wrong with this. In fact, it allows our business life to mirror the cycles of life by having time of abundance and times of clearing. Whatever your unique intent welcoming this success into your life and cultivating your magic practice beyond just your altar and home life yet welcoming the magic into all aspects of your life.

Chapter 10: Spells for Self Help

Especially in the pace of modern life with the ways of work, family and social life we often find ourselves in need of cultivating practices of self-help. Whether this be more self-esteem, rest, confidence, focus or just a moment to breathe. We can of course cultivate practices of regular sleeping patterns, eating right or exercising, yet we find we beat ourselves up when we miss out on these elements of life. So, as a Wiccan we can even call upon the magic of the elements to help cultivate these energies that help the rhythm of daily life.

Here as we explore various spells for cultivating this peace of mind. We are reminded the power of intent. For even if we are to cast these spells and then just merely sit back end except the magic to fall out of the sky, then we can often be disappointed in our spellcraft. There is a certain responsibility to cultivate also positive practices. Things like walking in nature, eating the right foods and more rest will only increase the power of our spell work.

For in this way we become closer to the elements that are assisting us by being in nature. We can feel the energy of the foods they are sending us that may hold the magic of the spells. Through sleep we even open ourselves to messages that may come in the form of dreams. So, this is some subtle ways we can even increase our magic and become a powerful spell caster. With this in mind let us begin to explore the subtly of our mind and improve our own well-being and cultivate practices to promote a healthy wise self.

Powerful Self-Empowerment Spell

This is a potent spell to improve self-esteem and confidence, ideally practice this spell daily until you feel you have the desired amount of confidence in your life to take on the world. This is level of confidence is also crucial element in all spell work, so this makes an excellent foundation for further practice of the craft.

You Require:

     1 Red candle

     Matches

     Orange or Lemon essential oil

     Yarrow herb

     Rhodonite or Rose Quartz crystal

Casting your spell:

1. Open your circle taking the time to set the intent of cultivating confidence.
2. Anoint your candle with the Orange/Lemon essential oil and sprinkle it with Yarrow herb.
3. Light the candle allowing the fragrance of the herbs fill your circle.
4. Taking the crystal pass it through the flame of your candle, reciting the following nine times:

"I AM Love,
I AM Power,
I AM Enough,
I AM Joy,
I AM Good."

5. Take the time to sit and watch the candle feeling this mantra fill your circle and being, until the candle burns out.
6. Repeat this spell as often as you need to increase self-esteem and confidence. Any time you feel low, simply pause take a moment to imagine your candle still burning and repeat this mantra internally. You will begin to notice the power flowing back into your being.

Note: This is what Wicca calls the "I AM mantra," this is a POWERFUL mantra to repeat at any time you need to increase your own confidence or will power. You can change the words to be "I AM inspiring, creative, respected, worthy, beautiful, or anything you wish to call into your life. This is working with our inner magic of reprogramming the subconscious and opening our vibration to these energies. If you believe this mantra and continue with regularity you will notice results come into your life fast, and the more you believe it the more powerful the results. This was one of my first spells and I even wrote this as an affirmation on my bathroom mirror, so I would always read it when I went in there to uplift myself. Other people started reading it also and saying how it was having an effect on their lives. Try this mantra anytime you are feeling low or need to raise your love.

Accepting Confidence Spell

A spell to help clear blockages from confidence and growing in self-worth. Any Wiccan whom struggles to accept confidence into their life or being, can benefit from casting this spell to allow more room to remove negative thought patterns and open one's self to a more confident enriched life.

You require:

1 White Candle

1 Candle holder

Paper and Pen

Casting your acceptance spell

1. Cast your circle and sit with your sacred space.
2. Take a moment to write down on the paper all the aspects you may find difficult to accept, taking the time you need to truly authentically reflect, the more truth you have the more you may open yourself to this flow. Next write down changes that you need to make but haven't made yet.
3. Light the candle and focus on the flicker flame.
4. As you watch this flame imagine yourself letting go of these traits, experiences and elements of yourself that you no longer need. Allow yourself to visualize a new life that is even better than you could imagine, opening yourself to all possibilities. Noticing limitless possibilities beginning to open for you from every direction and a pure light of love and peace filling your being.
5. Notice this sensation beginning to overtake your entire being, allowing this to expand beyond your wildest imagination and desire.

6. Watch as the flame dances and flickers as the candle continues to burn bright as this sensation continues to flood your being.

7. Continue to watch this flame for as long as you like. Before closing the circle and then leave the candle to burn all the way until it burns out by its own accord.

8. Once the candle has burnt out keep the wax as a reminder of this transformation, keeping it in a bag or space place to call upon when it is needed for more acceptance.

Liquid Confidence Essential Oil

An easy magical oil that you can make and apply to your heart or feet anytime you feel sensations of low self-esteem and wish to inflate your confidence. You can either massage the oil to your feet or heart or carry in your bag to inhale at any time. To make your own blend simple mix the following and keep in a small oil bottle.

2 Drops of Bergamot essential oil

2 Drops of Fennel essential oil

2 Drops of Frankincense essential oil

2 Drops Ylang Ylang essential oil

2 Drops of Geranium essential oil

Apply this oil any time you wish to call more luck into your life. Take three breaths as you apply the oil to allow the fragrance to flood your system and activate the magic of these herbs. To increase the potency, you can even recite the "I am mantra" that we discussed earlier out loud or mentally, calling forth any confidence you may need.

Turning over a new leaf spell

We often wish to change an old habit or break an unconscious pattern. Yet turning over a new leaf can often be a hard task and take time to cultivate the new habit. So, we can cultivate a little magic to help us turn over this new leaf! Perfect added boost when beginning a new resolution or in time for a new habit. This is also a perfect spell for a witch becoming more comfortable with their spellcasting and wishing to take it to the next level, however if you are a beginning witch do not be disheartened as you could even turn over a new leaf in your magic practice.

You will require:

    A green candle and holder

    A nail or athame for carving

    1 Bay leaf

Ink pen, be sure you can write on the bay leaf

4 small quartz crystals

Cauldron

Casting your spell:

1. Begin by cleansing all your magical items and casting a circle to hold space.
2. From here set you intent clearly in your minds eye. Continue to focus on your intent until you can visualize a sigil that represents your intent. Once you have this sigil carve this into the side of your candle. Copy this same sigil onto the Bay leaf with the pen.
3. Once you have prepared the candle and bay leaf, place the leaf in the center of the altar with the sigil facing down. Place the candle directing behind your bay leaf and ignite the flame as you do.
4. From here place your crystals at the four cardinal points of the altar.

Note: You have now set the space for your spell work, these are important to be sure the spell works and channels the magic in the right way, so take you time in these first stages.

5. Next take hold of your bay leaf, keeping your intent in your focus. Begin to flip the leaf over and over, flipping it towards yourself, until you complete seven rotations whilst reciting the following:

"This new leaf I turn and turn.
My new life begins right now."

6. Carefully burn your leaf in the flame of your candle and then throw your bay leaf into the cauldron. Allow the leaf to burn while you focus on the old habit burning away. Let the candle burn down slowly and safely.
7. Close your circle and move into your embrace your new ways. As challenges arise, take a moment to breathe and recall the sensation of the leaf in your hand and remember turning it over recalling your incantation, this will help you be guided into new ways.

Magical Inspiration Spell

In life it is not only important surround ourselves with inspire people, good foods and right movement yet also to cultivate this inspiration and creative energy within ourselves. This is a spell to spark those creative elements in your own life to allow you to access the same aspects of creativity that you respect in your role models, idols or muses. With this magic your daydreams will soon become into fruition. Simply through making collage poster that will act as a talisman to plant this seed of creativity into your subconscious and bring forth energy of the cosmos that assisted those before you to be in your favor!

You will require:

Yellow candle

Olive oil

Fresh thyme

Crushed jasmine leaves

Large poster paper

Scissors

Glue

Magazine cuttings, articles or book quotations

Bell

Spell preparation:

1. First begin by brainstorming on all your favorite muses and inspirations in life, this can be authors, poets,

speakers, musicians, family, friends, painters or any of the like.

2. Take time to then source any images or short quotations that trigger your memory of this person. Really allow your creativity to begin flowing at this point. From here begin to cut out these extracts and place them onto the poster paper.

3. Once you have glued them down onto the poster you will be ready to begin your spell.

Casting your spell:

1. Find a space for your posture where it can be seen easily when you are engaged in your creative flow. Prepare this space to for the posture to be hung at the end of your spell.

2. Take a moment to dress your candle, anointing it with the olive oil. Combine all your herbs and then roll the candle through the herbs, until it is thickly coated.

3. Place the candle in front of the collaged poster and ignite the wick. Simultaneously sparking your creativity.

4. Now ring the bell and recite the following whilst continuously ringing the bell:

"O' Muses, givers of joy and light,
Hearken now unto my plight.
Frozen blocks of thought be gone!
Remove obstacles from this moment on.
And cast away any obstructions far away
from me,
That stifle all forms of creativity.
Lend inspiration from above,
Infuse me with passion once undreamed of.
An inspiration to others I will become,
As I march to the beat of my own drum.

5. Once you have finished reciting this, place down the bell and leave the posture in front of the burning candle until the candle naturally burns out.
6. After the candle finishes burning place the posture into your desired space where you will see it whenever you engage in your creativity. Allowing the growing inspiration to flow through you every time you see this posture.

Motivation and Determination Spell

A brilliant spell for the Wiccan preparing to create their own spells and practice adopting their own flare into the craft. This spell is referred to as a *"Spiritual kick in the ass"* by many

Wiccans. Yet one key ingredient is that it resonates with you 100%, meaning if you need to adjust this spell over time or change something to suit your craft more, then this spell encourages and requires you to do so. Working with increasing your motivation and determination in projects of daily life or even long-term projects, this is a spell that can also be harnessed over time to increase the potency.

You will require:

> Yellow ritual candle
>
> Lemon juice
>
> Paper and pen
>
> Music that hypes you up

Casting your spell:

1. Prepare yourself for the spell by listening to your hype up music or dancing, moving around, shaking anything to get you in an excited space and state of mind. Cultivating this feeling of being fully energized, remember this feeling.

2. Open your circle and cultivate your sacred space, beginning to ground yourself yet remembering this energized sensation.

3. Carve into your candle the Raidho rune (x)

4. Then anoint your candle in lemon juice. As you do this focus on all the things in your life that you need motivation for.

5. Once your candle is ready, write a list of all these aspects of your life you want more motivation. Followed by folding the paper into a small square.

6. Placing the candle into a holder or fireproof space, to allow it to fully burn out. Light your candle and focus on the determination beginning to grow inside of you.

7. Speak the following to the spirits to call in their aid:

"Spirits assembled, bestow unto me a healthy dose of energy.
Help me dedicate my time to where it is truly needed
And transform my laziness into ambition.
So I speak, so mote it be."

8. Take a moment to focus on the movements of the flame and then seal the list using the candle wax.

9. Now sit with the sealed list and continue to watch the dancing flame. Remain in a meditative position feeling

the sensation of motivation and determination expanding inside of your being, visualizing all the things you need to do to complete your list. Any time thoughts, feelings or emotions arise of you not wanting to do something on the list visualize the fire burning it away and being replaced by the energized feeling you gained from dancing or listening to music.

10. Once the candle burns out sleep with this list under your pillow. Arise in the morning with a new sense of determination in life!

Positivity Peach Spell

The spell for the days when you are facing a challenging situation or low on energy and need the reinforcement of positive optimism. Working with the concept *"let thy food be thy medicine"* when we eat with intent that intent becomes our energy and focus. Thus, an enchanted peach for breakfast will bring more positivity into your life. Throughout history peaches have been seen as a sign of love, protection, fertility and immortality, along with all forms of luck and positive influence. We can even see the cheerful energy in the color of the peach.

You will only require in peach and athame.

Casting your spell:

1. Cleanse the peach before beginning the spell.
2. Using the athame carve your name into the skin of the peach.
3. As you do this take the time visualize yourself being filled with luck, joy, positivity and abundance.
4. Slowly and mindfully eat the peach. Feeling these sensations of love, optimism fill your being!
5. Bury the pip of the peach in your garden as you leave the house for the day.
6. Allow this positivity to radiate from your being throughout the entire day.

As you continue to grow and develop your confidence, focus and well-being you will inevitably begin to learn the secrets that exist behind this positive spellcraft. May these spells merely serve as a guide along you path to help build this foundation. With the vision and wish that in turn you will be able to bring greater well-being to others around you. Allow yourself the space and creativity to make these spells part of your Grimoire, with your own personal flare. For if you can begin to add your own variations and editions you will already be harnessing the power of the spell by feeling more inspired, creative and empowered with your magic. This is how tradition has grown throughout the years, as the secrets are passed down, each witch adds their own knowledge and wisdom thus refining and perfecting these ways of magic. Thank you for your contribution. Thank you for creating more magic within this world by continuing to practice and thank you for being as you are. May your wellness lead to the wellness and joy of all those you meet along the path.

Conclusion: Closing the Circle

Now as we come to a close on our journey of spells and magic together let us take a moment to acknowledge what we have begun to cultivate merely within sharing this knowledge together. Through this exploration and understanding of the types of magic you may encounter you can now begin to navigate your own path. To have the confidence that you may start your own Book of Shadows as you continue down the path. Now you can even discover which magical tools will best benefit your own practice, in the same way that Gerald Gardner or Robert Cochrane found their own truth within the Wiccan art, may you now find your expression and truth. Thank you for taking this time to begin your exploration. Whilst you may decide to identify or not as a Wicca, witch, pagan or any title, the sharing of this knowledge by the many leads to the sharing of magic between all of life.

It is the wish, as shared already, that these pages may serve but as a guide for you to begin your magical journey and connection to spell casting. Keeping in mind that the true magic is already within you. Now it is time to activate this magic, listen to your inner wisdom, trust the omens that arise and fall.

Develop and become more sensitive and while listening to this inner intuition will guide you along the path from an initiate Wiccan to and adept whom is creating their own spells and rituals in no time. First learn and decide which type of witchcraft resonates with you. Then find you tools of the craft. Honor these truths, they will truly help you cultivate true magic. Remember to record your progress, notice what works and what can be refined- and give space for grace! Time will be your friend, just relax into the magic. When we cultivate this faith and acceptance of time, space and divine grace we notice how rapidly our spell work and practice propels forth.

Whether you are casting spells of love, for business and abundance, general well-being or positivity, or possibly even cleansing the past to move forward, continue your practice. There may even be times when your spells do not work straight away or even at all. This is perfectly ok! The greatest of witches also had to make these mistakes along the path, had to make adjustments, refinements and rework the kinks out of their spell work. Yet, this is often where the magic happens! Think of Doreen Valiente situation, she tried many various covens- even started her own. Whilst she ultimately left each way, failed starting her own and turned to be a ley finder, we still recall her fondly as the *Mother of Wicca*. Share this wisdom and honesty about your spells working or not working yet be not disheartened the magic will come in time and flourish within your life.

If you can learn to adopt these techniques and spells may the ways of old come to you in abundance. You may wish to trade these ways with other witches you meet in your local community or even, if you are a *Tech Witch,* online. This is a grand way to allow your wisdom to grow and bloom. However, as you cast a spell, keep this your own secret until you see the spell come to its end. This is also a key to the magic, for the more people that know the more energy the spell has to move through. At times we use this to our advantage by casting collective spells. However, for this form of magic we must completely have faith and trust in those we are casting with. Being completely sure of their intent. So, for your own personal spellcraft cast in private, document your own results and then share when the time has come to fruition. Again, this will allow the collective community of Wicca and magic evolve, as was the dream of the founders from this magic tradition.

With much appreciation gratitude and love, thank you for reading this Wiccan Book of Spells. Enjoy the unfolding of magic in your life, and may it serve you to see all magic in life, as it has for myself. Let us acknowledge The Goddess, The God and the Elements- *Fire, Air, Water, Earth and Spirit,* may they continue to guide us and unite us. We give thanks to those before us lighting the way and keeping the ways of old alive and true. Now the time has come for you to write your own Book of Shadows, to connect to your own Grimoire, Craft and wise ways. So, as I leave you here, I will close with this final parting blessing:

May the magic in your soul, continue to unfold.

May the words of truth, keep your heart in youth.

May the magic that we see, allow you to be free.

I say unto you, that wisdom moves in all you do.

Trust the ways of old, for this is how love is told.

Allow love and truth to guide you in light, love and all you need.

So, mote it be. So, mote it be.

So, mote it be.

WICCA
HERBAL MAGIC

A COMPLETE GUIDE TO THE NATURAL MAGIC OF HERBS, FLOWERS AND ESSENTIAL OILS.
THE ULTIMATE BOOK OF SHADOWS FOR PRACTICING WICCAN HERBAL MAGIC

ATHENA CROWLEY

Printed in Great Britain
by Amazon

36204553R00099